The American Market for Manufactured Exports from the Developing Countries

Albert H. Small

The Praeger Special Studies program—
utilizing the most modern and efficient book
production techniques and a selective
worldwide distribution network—makes
available to the academic, government, and
business communities significant, timely
research in U.S. and international economic, social, and political development.

The American Market for Manufactured Exports from the Developing Countries

Praeger Publishers New York Washington London

PRAEGER SPECIAL STUDIES IN INTERNATIONAL ECONOMICS AND DEVELOPMENT

PRAEGER PUBLISHERS
111 Fourth Avenue, New York, N.Y. 10003, U.S.A.
5, Cromwell Place, London S.W.7, England

Published in the United States of America in 1972
by Praeger Publishers, Inc.

Library of Congress Catalog Card Number: 70-180853

Printed in the United States of America

The furor that followed the imposition, in August, 1971, of a 10 percent surcharge on U.S. imports obscured other tariff issues, and rightly so. In one action, the United States, temporarily at least, wiped out the results of years, in some cases of decades, of tariff-reducing negotiations. Even the 50 percent rate cuts of the Kennedy Round were probably in most cases considerably less than the amount of the surcharge.

It will be interesting to observe the effect of the surcharge upon the level of U.S. imports, as well as changes in monetary relationships resulting from the "floating" of the dollar. It seems inevitable that the increase in this level will be arrested to some degree, but there may be some surprises for those who believe the surcharge effects will be drastic or uniform. In the case of many manufactured products, ranging from binoculars to miniature electronic calculators, U.S. purchasers are probably almost as dependent on foreign supplies as they are for such raw products as green coffee; in other instances, domestic industry may be either unwilling or unable to assume a very much larger role in supplying demand than it played before the surcharge.

If demand for imports proves thus to be relatively inelastic, this may be a demonstration of what the author has long suspected: that sales of most manufactured products are much more strongly influenced by marketing accomodations than by simple price mechanics. Often, when involved in international conferences where the object of discussion was to achieve a reduction of some percentage points in the tariff rate, the author has mused on the inefficacy of such reductions unaccompanied by appropriate marketing efforts. In contrast, imports of products have frequently risen rapidly even in the face of moderate tariff increases, presumably because effective marketing techniques were being employed.

The author, having over a decade of experience as a marketing consultant, is familiar with the varying sales results achieved with adequate marketing techniques. For example, two advertisements for the same product at the same price placed in the same magazine can draw sales results in the ratio of twenty to one, depending on the effectiveness of the advertising copy used.

It has long been the author's desire to relate the importance of effective marketing to the attainment of the export goals of the developing countries. The opportunity to apply himself systematically to this task was furnished by the challenge of preparing a dissertation (from which this book is drawn) at the American University's School of Business Administration. It is hoped that these resulting efforts may merit some consideration from those who, either as practitioners or observers of the export trade of the developing countries, are similarly interested in its expansion.

Over the several years between the conception of this idea and its present execution, many have aided with encouragement, suggestions, advice, and criticism. The author wishes most particularly to pay homage to Howe Martyn, a business man turned academician, whose writings have so effectively illuminated many aspects of today's international business world and who, as Director of the University's International Business Program, inspired and guided this work, and also to other members of the Dissertation Advisory Committee, Drs. Frank Holloway, Gangadhar Kori, Myles Robinson, and Wilson Scott, who patiently wrestled with the drafts and redirected the manuscript where its essential aim was blunted. The final responsibility, however; must rest with the author, who takes particular pains to caution the reader that what follows on these pages is in no way, directly or indirectly, the official view of the U.S. government or of any of its agencies.

CONTENTS

Page

PREFACE   v

LIST OF TABLES   xi

LIST OF FIGURES   xii

Chapter

1   INTRODUCTION   3

    The Problem of Research and Supporting
        Problems   3
    Limitations   4
    Probable Value and Importance of Study   5
    Methodology   8
    The Data   9
    Definitions   9
    Organization of the Study   12
    Notes   12

2   TRENDS IN U.S. MANUFACTURED IMPORTS
    FROM THE DEVELOPING COUNTRIES   17

    Exports of the Developing Countries   17
    U.S. Imports from the Developing
        Countries   18
        Manufactured Imports from the SDCs   24
        Chemical Imports from the SDCs   27
        Imports of Manufactures Classified by
            Material from the SDCs   27
        Machinery and Transport Equipment Im-
            ports from the SDCs   32
        Miscellaneous Manufactured Imports
            from the SDCs   32
        Processed Food Imports from the SDCs   33
    Relationship Between Manufactured SDC Ex-
        ports and Total SDC Exports   35

Chapter   Page

        Summary   38
        Notes   39

3   DEMAND FACTORS FOR MANUFACTURED
     IMPORTS   43

        Price Versus Nonprice Demand Factors   43
        Manufactured Imports and Product Differ-
          entiation   44
        The Role of Tariffs   45
        The Importer-Exporter Relationship   51
        Marketing Knowledge as a Limiting
          Factor in Types of Manufactured Im-
          ports   55
        Summary   56
        Notes   57

4   DESIGNING FOR THE AMERICAN MARKET   61

        The Design is the Product   61
        Impulse Sales: Purchase Optionality
          Illustrated   67
        The Relationship of Design and Function   67
        "New" Products   69
        Design Mortality   70
        The Degree of Design Distinctiveness   71
        Summary   74
        Notes   75

5   QUALITY ISSUES FOR THE AMERICAN
     MARKET   79

        The Quality Crisis in the U.S. Market   79
        The Quality Opportunity for Imported
          Goods   80
        Quality as a Matter of Ability   81
        Quality as a Matter of Policy   84
        Quality as a Matter of Consistency   84
        Quality as a Matter of Management   86
        Quality Marks and Quality Standards   87
        The Rise of Consumerism   89
        Summary   91
        Notes   92

Chapter   Page

6   PACKING AND PACKAGING MANUFAC-
     TURED EXPORTS FOR THE AMERICAN
     MARKET   95

        The Distinction Between Packing and
           Packaging   95
        Innovative Packing for Manufactured
           Exports   96
        Materials and Know-How Problems in
           Packing   97
        Packaging and Channels of Distribution   101
        Packaging Problems   103
        How the Package Sells   105
        Current Packaging Trends   107
        Legal Requirements for Packaging and
           Labeling   108
        Summary   111
        Notes   112

7   ISSUES CONNECTED WITH DISTRIBUTION
     CHANNELS   117

        Distribution: Pathway from Producer to
           End-User   117
        Mass-Merchandising Versus Specialist
           Importers   119
        Industrial Importers   123
        Market Segmentation   125
        Exclusivity   134
        Pricing Margins   135
        The Role of Sales Promotion in Distri-
           bution   136
        Summary   138
        Notes   139

8   THE COMMUNICATION PROBLEM AND EX-
     PORTER DEPENDABILITY   143

        The Exporter-Importer Relationship   143
        The Technicalities of Trade   144
        The Communication Problem   146
        Importer Reactions to the Communication
           Problem   151

Chapter   Page

      International Clearinghouse for New Im-
        ports   152
      Summary   154
      Notes   155

9   FINDINGS AND CONCLUSIONS   159

      Findings   159
      Conclusions   165
      Notes   168

APPENDIX A   173

APPENDIX B   177

BIBLIOGRAPHY   179

ABOUT THE AUTHOR   191

LIST OF TABLES

Table   Page

1   U.S. Imports from SDCs, 1964 and 1970   20

2   U.S. Imports from SDCs, by Region   22

3   SDCs from Which Half or More of U.S. Imports
     Were of Section 3 Products, 1970   25

4   Proportions of U.S. Imports from SDCs, by Type of
     Product, 1964 and 1970   26

5   Proportion of Manufactured Products in U.S. Imports
     from SDCs, 1970, and Percentage Point Change
     from 1964   28

6   SDCs from Which U.S. Imported $1 Million or More of
     Chemicals, by Category, 1970   30

7   SDCs from Which U.S. Imported $10 Million or More
     of SITC Section 6 Goods, 1970, Total and by Selec-
     ted Category   31

8   SDCs from Which U.S. Imported $1 Million or More of
     Section 7 Goods, 1970, Total and by Category   33

9   SDCs from Which U.S. Imported $2 Million or More of
     Section 8 Goods, in 1970 and Distribution by Selected
     Category   34

10   U.S. Imports of Processed Foods from SDCs, 1970   36

11   SDCs from Which Imports and Manufactured Imports
     Grew Most Rapidly, 1964-70   37

12   Food Consumption: Calories per Day per Capita   63

13   Newsprint Consumption: Kilograms per Capita per
     Year   64

14   Imports of Wood Products from SDCs Compared with
     Total U.S. Imports from SDCs, 1968   98

Table   Page

15   Cost of Packaging, Selected Products   106

16   Standard Package-Size Agreements Secured by the
      Department of Commerce, January, 1970   110

17   Principal Products Imported from Less-Developed
      Countries Under U.S. Tariff Section 807, 1969   124

18   Industries with Inputs from Iron-and-Steel-Foundries
      Industry   126

19   U.S. Customs Districts with Largest Aggregate Cus-
      toms Duty Collections, June 30, 1969   131

LIST OF FIGURES

Figure   Page

1   Cost and Margin Relationships Between Importer
      and New Source of Supply   54

2   Checklist for Screening American Market Opportuni-
      ties for Manufactured Exports from the Developing
      Countries   164

Appendix Figure

1   Theoretical Effect of Cost Reduction Stemming from
      Preferential Tariff Reduction on Supply-Demand-
      Price Relationships Under Perfect Competition   177

The American Market for Manufactured Exports from the Developing Countries

INTRODUCTION

THE PROBLEM OF RESEARCH AND
SUPPORTING PROBLEMS

How improved marketing methods can be used to increase manufactured imports by the United States from developing countries is the problem that forms the basis of this study. This general problem can be divided into a number of major component problems:

1. The ability of suppliers in developing countries to achieve and maintain quality acceptable for the American market

2. The ability of suppliers in developing countries to furnish products of a design to meet the tastes and desires of the American buyer

3. The issue of adopting packing and packaging procedures and techniques meeting the requirements of the American market

4. Channels of distribution if market penetration is to succeed

5. The manner in which sales promotion in the U.S. market can be performed

6. The relation of pricing policy to distribution

7. The degree to which current export-import procedures are an obstacle to the expansion of manufactured imports from the developing countries

8. The effect of communications and other problems due
   to geographic and cultural distances on the willingness
   of importers to depend on exporters.

At the conclusion of the above subinvestigations, this study will
endeavor to distill the findings as a way of developing conclusions for
practical action recommendations.

LIMITATIONS

Imports of manufactured products from the developing countries
are constrained by the ability of such countries to produce manufactured
goods. A constellation of forces limits this manufacturing ability.
The developing countries are poorly endowed with the technological
knowledge required to produce many types of manufactured goods
and with the assortment of production and management skills required
to man plants of the types required. But more important, developing
countries lack the capital for constructing and equipping the necessary
industries. The lack of capital, typically considered the key problem
of their national development, can be broadly attributed to three
factors: a lack of adequate domestic savings produced by their economies (and some hesitancy on the part of private domestic capitalists
to invest in productive enterprises in their own countries); finite
limits to the amount of capital being made available from the developed
countries in the form of investment, aid, and aid-type loans; and
inadequacies in the ability of developing countries to secure the capital
in exchange for their own exports. Economists have frequently referred
to this final problem as the "trade gap."[1]

Administered barriers to international trade present another
formidable series of hurdles for imports of manufactured products
from the developing countries. Although tariffs have long been cited
as the traditional barrier to international trade, U.S. tariffs have been
reduced substantially during the decades since World War II.[2] "Effective" rather than "nominal" tariffs are believed by some to be the real
barriers, however, and tariff-alleviation proposals for the developing
countries are being widely discussed. This topic is considered in
Chapter 3, in connection with price-competitive factors affecting
imports from the developing countries.

In addition to tariffs, quotas and other quantitative limitations
or prohibitions are also employed. The use of quotas is of greatest
significance in the textile field. In general, quotas, such as those
applying to cotton textiles, set a ceiling on the amount of a manufactured

product that can be imported into the United States. Absolute prohibitions against import are of chief significance in connection with
health regulations. Beef, for example, cannot be imported (unless
canned) from countries with cattle hoof-and-mouth disease, and this
includes most potential Latin American suppliers.[3]

While the limitation of the study to marketing omits many of
these meaningful spheres of importability, the study suffers from
problems of scope because of its broadness as well. Dealing in a
single study with all types of manufactured goods, produced by varying
techniques, from diverse materials, for capital or consumer use, and
sold by a wide range of distributive methods, involves a burden of
range on the useful findings that may be adduced. The countries that
must be included are located on four continents in both hemispheres
and their physical and cultural endowments vary widely. While there
are definite evolutions of marketing practice in the United States,
no "one best way" exists to sell most products. Different approaches,
different types of outlets, and different buyer psychologies are all
successfully employed by different sellers.[4]

PROBABLE VALUE AND IMPORTANCE OF STUDY

Notwithstanding the limitations just cited, the study should
produce findings of value. The need of the developing nations to
increase their manufactured exports (and, by extension, for the United
States, the world's largest single national market, to increase such
imports) has been widely accepted by writers in the various political,
economic, and business fields concerned with the development of such
countries. To summarize the generally accepted arguments:

1. Industrialization is the prime source of increasing
   national wealth.

2. These countries have a shortage of funds to industri-
   alize.

3. Export expansion accordingly becomes essential as a
   way of helping to alleviate this shortage.

4. Such expansion must involve manufactured exports
   because exports of primary commodities are not
   expandable at will.

Reinforcing the above arguments is the belief by many specialists in the field that industrialization needs export markets at least temporarily just in order to survive until national income has grown sufficiently to provide the necessary home-market demand.

Expressed in its simplest terms, the desire of a developing country to "develop" is a desire to multiply the product of the nation's labor by the capacity of the machine. It is a desire to transform the economy from low-capital-using means of production to high-capital-using means of production. Only in this way can the country hope to raise per capita national product to the level of the presently industrialized countries.

Industrialization—the creation of a range of national industries— is considered the sine qua non of this development.[5] While it may be theoretically possible for a country simply to apply capital to its extractive occupations and thus so effectively to produce and export primary products that the wide range of industrial products that characterize a developed country can be purchased from abroad, this has never in fact happened. Even developed countries like Denmark, Canada, and Australia, whose specialized primary exports are a major characteristic of their economies, still derive well under 20 percent of their national product from primary-product production.[6] The excessive transport cost alone would probably make unlikely a country's economic development to a high per capita income stage without substantial local industry.

The full development of industrialization among the western countries typically occupied periods of half a century.[7] This fact alone would raise the question of how developing countries are to convert from low industrialization to high industrialization within the time span that their aspirations call for, without massive influxes of capital. As previously mentioned, this capital comes from limited sources, and some of these sources, such as foreign aid and aid-related loans and grants, actually appear to have been declining in recent years.[8]

So the developing countries are faced with the need to expand exports. The fruitlessness of this quest with respect to many primary materials is self-evident. The homogeneity of many primary products and their autonomous rate of usage threatens to bankrupt exporting nations that expand their exports to the point that aggregate supply begins to depress world prices. Demand limitations for some products, such as coffee, are painfully evident, and others, such as basic metals, continually face the threat of abundance because of substitutions and use-economization. Use-economization (e.g., the use of less tin in solder), which is induced by high prices, sometimes prevents the reexpansion of demand when prices lower.[9]

The net result of all of the foregoing is that the major hope for expansion of exports of the developing nations shifts to manufactured products. Such expansion has actually occurred to a remarkable degree, as discussed in Chapter 2. But the development goals of the developing countries indicate no lessening of interest or desire for further and faster expansion of such exports.

Still another reason can be found for the desire of the developing countries to expand their exports of manufactured products. Such countries see the route to industrialization, at least initially, in terms of two principal paths—import substitution or export expansion. The key to both these routes is the establishment of the market without which industry cannot maintain itself. The import-substitution path attempts to secure this market by taking over the market in the country currently served by imports. Fundamentally, this approach has two limitations. The existing market for manufactured products is often disappointingly limited because of the low level of income in the country. And pressing import substitution too quickly results in the "forced-draft" initiation of many industrial projects whose low level of efficiency can be protected only by stringent import restrictions. The resulting high real cost of industrial products not only dissipates the country's resources but may threaten its entire export efficiency. The "cost" of a country's exports is determined, after all, not only by the cost of the direct inputs, such as materials and supplies, but also by the cost of the consumption goods that must be purchased by those employed in the exporting industry.[10]

To sum up, the incentives to increase exports of manufactured products are so great and the problems so many that any approach offering help in this quest is well worth exploring. Improved marketing is one such approach. Marketing is, after all, a modern technology in the same sense that steelmaking is, to be created or to be transferred from efficient practitioners in the field. But unlike steelmaking, the capital requirements for better marketing range from nil to modest levels, when compared with most other advanced technologies.

It should be noted that there has been a reasonable amount of attention in recent marketing literature to problems associated with the achievement of efficient marketing within the developing countries.[11] The literature relating to export marketing of these countries has been limited, however, consisting largely of the publications of the General Agreement on Tariffs and Trade/U.N. Conference on

Trade and Development (GATT/UNCTAD) International Trade Center in Geneva, and only a minor portion of this output has dealt with marketing of exports for the United States. It is, therefore, felt that the present study can represent a significant contribution to the field.

Parenthetically, note may be made of the value to the United States, other than altruistic, of the growth and development of the economies of the developing countries. Economic history has indicated that the growth of a nation's purchasing power is associated with the growth of its demand for imports. The contrast may be drawn in Britain's relationships with India and the United States. In both cases, the relationship was at one time that of a developed country with an underdeveloped country. But today the United States has developed and takes Britain's exports at the rate of over $2 billion annually (1969), whereas India, notwithstanding its much greater population, has yet fully to develop and takes less than $150 million annually of British exports.[12] The implication is clear: as the developing countries develop they should become much greater markets for U.S. exports, with consequent benefit to the U.S. economy and the American people.

METHODOLOGY

The approach of this study is to compare certain marketing methods that have been successfully used in the United States for manufactured products with marketing methods that have been used for manufactured imports from the developing countries. The differences between the two types of methods are used to derive conclusions as to improvements that may expand the imports in question. Historical data from both primary and secondary sources are used.

The study begins with a statistical analysis of the nature of recent imports of manufactured goods from the developing countries to indicate the nature, source, and rate of growth of such imports. This is followed by an analysis of the price and nonprice influences on demand for manufactured imports from the developing countries, with particular attention to the importance of tariffs in comparison with other marketing factors. Marketing factors are then dealt with one by one: the design of the product; its quality; its packing and packaging; factors affecting the choice of distributive channels, including distributive pricing and the problem of sales promotion; and finally, issues related to the exporter-importer relationship, especially the relationship of communication to business confidence.

THE DATA

The sources of information on currently successful marketing techniques in the United States abound in both book and periodical literature, and the beginning of a literature dealing with the export efforts of the developing countries has been alluded to. For primary data, however, the writer has concentrated upon American importers of manufactured products, since they are the necessary link between the producer in the developing country and the U.S. end user. Very little appears in print about the experiences of such firms. Some of these importers are specialists who sell only to wholesalers of a particular type of product; others are integrated all the way through to the home or business consumer.

The principal quantitative data used in this study are the U.S. import statistics, as published in the regular and special reports of the U.S. Census Bureau and other federal agencies. In addition, for comparative purposes, U.N. compilations of trade statistics of all countries, as well as special studies of U.N. affiliated agencies, such as GATT, are used. A variety of secondary sources, ranging from books that represent recognized standards in the marketing field to periodical articles, are among the secondary sources used. These are primarily American in origin.

For primary data, extensive contacts have been made with American importers, by personal interviews, telephone inquiries, and correspondence. These importers have reported on their experiences in bringing in or attempting to bring in manufactured goods from the developing countries, and they have furnished, at the request of the author, case histories to illustrate their general statements. Whenever possible, the writer has secured the original materials behind such case histories, ranging from importers' correspondence with their sources to samples of the materials involved in the trading.

DEFINITIONS

The definition of "manufactured good" presented special problems. All types of products in commerce, after all, represent some degree of processing from their original, raw, or extractive states. Green coffee and crude rubber will serve as illustrations of this point: each product requires elaborate collection and preparation phases before it is suitable for shipment in international trade.

Following United Nations statistical practice, the quantitative representation of manufactured goods has been primarily products classified
in Standard International Trade Classifications (SITC) 5 through 8,
which includes chemicals, manufactured goods classified chiefly by
material, machinery and transport equipment, and miscellaneous
manufactured articles.

The major omission of manufactured goods from this coverage
is processed food products, which are classified within SITC Group O.
Accordingly, separate studies of the statistics in this area are included,
and in the qualitative part of the study such products are included
wherever information on them was obtained.

Since the study deals with the origination of innovative exports
from a group of countries that have not in the past been major suppliers
of such imports, the definition of "developing countries" required
particular consideration. Countries were selected for inclusion in
this definition in the following manner: all countries classified in
Group II ("developing countries") in United Nations statistics were
considered. These countries are found in Latin America, the Middle
East, Africa (except South Africa), and Asia (except Japan); they do
not include Australia or New Zealand.

In the quantitative section of the study, all these countries were
used unless political changes made statistical trend verification impossible over the 1964-70 period studied. In addition, only independent
countries and countries from which U.S. imports were of a given size
were used; as explained in Chapter 2, these techniques were felt to
minimize certain possible types of bias, Nonetheless, in the qualitative part of the study, all countries are considered to the extent that
experience with their imports was felt to shed light on the problems
of the selected countries. For example, although Hong Kong is not
independent, some of its current problems are considered quite anala-
gous to those of Taiwan. Even European countries like Spain and
Greece are considered from time to time because some of their manufactured exports are felt to be still in the innovative situation dealt
with in the study. Past references from a country like Japan are
included where these may serve to illuminate the types of development
required by the presently developing countries.

The definition that imposes perhaps the most significant para-
meter upon the study is that of "marketing." Definitions of marketing
range from the narrow to the broad. Narrow definitions generally
limit marketing to the process of conveying goods and services from
producer to consumer and carefully differentiate "production" from

"marketing." Typically, the basis for this distinction is that production changes the form of materials. Broader definitions consider
marketing as encompassing all activities that affect economic transactions.[13] The distinction between the broad and narrow can be seen in
the case of product design. Since this is an integral part of production,
the narrow definition would exclude it; yet it obviously has a profound
effect on the sale of the article produced.

This study utilizes a broad definition of marketing, since the
purpose is to focus on those decisions and activities of management
that can increase the sale of manufactured imports from the primary-
commodity-exporting countries. At the same time, two limiting
features are added to the definition:

1. Marketing is limited to those activities that are possible with the existing level of production capabilities
   in these countries.

2. Marketing is defined as excluding the activities of
   government or quasi-government groups that seek
   to increase the sale of goods by changing the legal
   or economic parameters of the market.

The first limitation, for example, would not consider as marketing a change in production technology that made possible the production
of plywood instead of veneers; but the selection of different species
of locally available woods for veneering on the basis of end-user
preference would be considered marketing. The second limitation
would focus the marketing definition of this study on those activities
of economic enterprises (presumably, usually private enterprises)
that increase the volume of sale in the normal free-market way.
Excluded, for example, would be combinations that sought to raise
the price or limit the accomodations offered through an association
of exporters or activities to influence government export or import
regulations for the benefit of sellers.

In sum, then, the marketing definition of this study encompasses
all activities taken by sellers of manufactured imports from the developing countries to increase the sales of such products, except those
that involve changes in the existing level of production capability in
the originating country or those that seek to change the conditions
of the market through government or quasi-government actions.

ORGANIZATION OF THE STUDY

The study begins with an analysis, essentially statistical, of the volume, type, and origin of U.S. manufactured imports from selected developing countries, tracing changes that have occurred since 1964, depicting the ranking of individual countries and regions within the over-all group chosen for analysis, and contrasting these statistics with general figures for the countries classified by the United Nations as "developing."

This is followed by a discussion of the factors that can be demonstrated or may be surmised to influence the growth of such imports. Attention is directed to the influences encompassed within the definition of marketing just described. In contrast to conventional supply-demand analysis, the importance of nonprice competition (and its link to product differentiation) is emphasized. Following this, phases of marketing are treated under these major points of analysis: product design; product quality; packing and packaging; distribution channels; sales promotion; pricing policy; technical import barriers; and exporter-importer relationships.

It should be emphasized that the presentation of this study is by no means intended to denigrate or deny the importance of nonmarketing factors in promoting imports of manufactured goods from the developing countries. The effort is only to show that adequate effort on those factors encompassed within the definition of this study can yield results whether or not other factors are successfully dealt with.

NOTES

1. "These missing elements [which would make economic development possible], on the identity of which there is a good deal of agreement, are modern technical knowledge or know-how, capital, specially trained manpower, and a sound plan for using capital, manpower and technical knowledge." J. K. Galbraith, Economic Development in Perspective (Cambridge, Mass.: Harvard University Press, 1962), p. 6. A discussion of the historical problems of finding entrepreneurs for the export industries of the developing countries is found in Jonathan Levin, The Export Economies (Cambridge, Mass.: Harvard University Press, 1960), pp. 154-64. Problems of developing an industrial labor force are dealt with in Clark Kerr et al., Industrialization and Industrial Man (Cambridge, Mass.: Harvard University Press, 1960), pp. 165-81.

2. "The average tariff paid on dutiable U.S. imports dropped from 54 percent in 1933 to 12 percent in 1963. It has been estimated that about half of this reduction resulted from negotiated tariff reductions while the other half was due to the impact of inflation on specific duties." Ernest Preeg, Traders and Diplomats (Washington, D.C.: The Brookings Institution, 1970), p. 15. U.S. tariff rates on manufactured goods were again cut in the Kennedy Round negotiations concluded in 1967. Ibid., p. 208. For a perspective on the Kennedy Round, see Howe Martyn, "The Kennedy Round and U.S. Power," Dissent, May-June, 1968, pp. 259-61; and Howe Martyn, "After the Kennedy Round: The Regional Blocs Consolidate," Dalhousie Review, Autumn, 1968, pp. 312-23.

3. See U.S. Tariff Commission, Quantitative Import Restrictions of the United States (Washington, D.C.: Tariff Commission Publication 243, 1968). The United States is far from alone in maintaining quantitative restrictions: "A substantial proportion of manufactured exports from low-income countries to developed countries continues to be restricted by quotas. Excluding petroleum products, base metals, and ships . . . no less than 30 percent of manufactured goods are subject to quantitative restrictions. Cotton textiles and clothing and processed foodstuffs are subject to such restrictions in most wealthy countries. In addition, a number impose restrictions on noncotton textiles, leather and leather articles, footwear, dyestuffs, glass and glassware." Commission for the International Bank for Reconstruction and Development, Partners in Development (New York: Praeger, 1969), p. 137.

4. Perhaps the classic case of the company with unique methods in the American market has been the Hershey Chocolate Company, which built up a business with annual sales exceeding $200 million, selling consumer products without advertising. R. J. Holloway and R.S. Hancock, Marketing in a Changing Environment (New York: John Wiley & Sons, 1968), p. 359.

5. The link between industrialization and development has been stressed in writing on development for many decades. See, for example, K. Mandelbaum, The Industrialization of Backward Areas (Oxford: Basil Blackwell, 1947), pp. 1-2; and Alan Mountjoy, Industrialization and Under-Developed Countries (London: Hutchinson University Library, 1963), pp. 65-66. John Pincus, Trade, Aid and Development (New York: McGraw-Hill, 1967), p. 170, puts it this way: "An economically advanced economy is one that can perform a wide variety of complex economic functions. As a country develops, it introduces an ever larger variety of industries, financial agencies

and services. While a Switzerland, a Denmark, or a Belgium, because of its small population, makes no effort to produce everything, it is also true that such countries produce an ever wider variety of manufactures. If development essentially consists in building up both the variety of productive sectors and the level of output per worker, then export specialization can only be part of the story; domestic industrialization must play a major role."

6. Based on calculations from U.S., Department of Commerce, Bureau of International Commerce., Basic Data on the Economy of . . . (Washington, D.C.: U.S. Government Printing Office, various years). Specific identifications are as follows: Australia, OBR 63-38, 1963, p. 5; Canada, OBR 67-98, 1968, p. 6; and Denmark, OBE 68-84, 1968, p. 4.

7. If the period of industrialization is considered the time between Rostow's "take-off" and "maturity," this involved about half a century for Britain, France, and the United States and somewhat less for Germany, Sweden, and Japan. Transition from "maturity" to "high mass-consumption" took more than an additional 50 years for Britain, but only 10 to 30 years for the other countries. Canada and Australia, however, are experiencing take-off, maturity, and high mass-consumption almost simultaneously. W. W. Rostow, The Stages of Economic Growth (Cambridge, Eng.: The University Press, 1967), p. xiii.

8. Commission for the International Bank for Reconstruction and Development, Partners in Development (New York: Praeger, 1969), p. 137.

9. The drawbacks of primary products for export expansion are treated in United Nations, Proceedings of the United Nations Conference on Trade and Development, Vol. IV: Trade in Manufactures (New York, 1964), pp. 136-37.

10. Murray Bryce, Policies and Methods for Industrial Development (New York: McGraw-Hill, 1965), pp. 70-71; and H. B. Lary, Imports of Manufactures from Less Developed Countries (New York: National Bureau of Economic Research, 1968), pp. 10-11.

11. This remedies a previous lack. "Until recently," wrote Reed Moyer in 1965, "marketing has been almost totally neglected in the literature on economic development." Reed Moyer, Marketing in Economic Development (East Lansing: Institute for International Business Management Studies, Michigan Stage University, Occasional Paper No. 1, 1965), p. 1.

12. Organization for Economic Cooperation and Development, Trade by Commodities—Market Summaries, Series C, Vol. I: General, January-December 1969 (Paris, 1970), pp. 106-7.

13. Charles F. Phillips and Delbert J. Duncan, Marketing Principles and Methods (6th ed.; Homewood, Ill.: R. D. Irwin, 1968), p. 3, refer to marketing as "the bridge between production and consumption," based on the work of Lockley and McInnes and excluding activities that involve a significant change in the form of goods. In comparison with this narrow definition, W. J. Taylor and R. T. Shaw, Jr., Marketing: An Integrated Analytical Approach (2d ed.; Cincinnati, Ohio: South-Western Publishing Co., 1969), p. 4, quote the American Marketing Association definition of marketing as "the performance of business activities that direct the flow of goods and services from producer to consumer or user" and back this up with illustrations of such activities as product innovation. Another example of a broad definition is that of Wroe Alderson in Perry Bliss, ed., Marketing and the Behavioral Sciences (Boston: Allyn and Bacon, Inc., 1963), pp. 26-27. Mr. Alderson views marketing as all the necessary transformations in heterogeneous supplies through the process of sorting to match the purchaser's need. Refining and retailing are thus both encompassed.

EXPORTS OF THE DEVELOPING COUNTRIES

"Unprecedented" describes the growth of world trade in the years since the end of World War II. The term applies not only to the levels of trade achieved but also to the sustained rate of growth. The last absolute decline in world trade occurred in 1958. By 1968, after a decade of uninterrupted growth, world exports reached almost $240 billion, well over twice the 1958 level.[1] And the rate of growth appears to be accelerating.

Thus, between 1950 and 1965, world exports grew at the rate of 7.4 percent annually. Between 1965 and 1966, world exports rose 9 percent and between 1966 and 1967, 5 percent. The slower rate of growth is attributable to the dampening effect of approximately simultaneous recessions in the United States and Germany, but between 1967 and 1968 world exports jumped 11 percent.[2] In 1969, they were almost 14 percent higher than in 1968.[3]

The over-all growth rates of world trade conceal, however, disparities in trade growth between the wealthier industrialized nations and the poorer nations whose industrialization is minor or nil. During the period 1963-68, when world exports had been increasing some 55 percent, exports of the industrialized nations grew almost 64 percent, but exports of the nations categorized by the United Nations as "developing" grew only 37 percent.[4]

Against this generally bleak picture of trade growth for the nonindustrialized countries, one element has been somewhat brighter. Processed or manufactured exports of such countries have been growing rapidly.[5] Between 1963 and 1968, when over-all exports of the

developing countries increased 37 percent, their exports of manufactured goods increased 97 percent. Even in 1968, however, manufactured
exports[6] constituted less than one quarter of the total exports of the
developing countries versus three quarters for the industrialized
countries.[7]

One analyst has pointed out that developing countries have
frequently been more successful in expanding their "minor" exports
than their "major" ones. The major exports are the traditional primary
products of the country, for which the country itself may be a large
factor in the international supply, e.g., Malaysian tin or Brazilian
green coffee. The minor export may be agricultural—the example of
tomatoes from Mexico is cited—but it is quite frequently a manufactured
or at least a processed good.[8]

Manufactured exports of the developing countries may have been
increasing at an annual rate as much as three times that previously
anticipated—at a rate as high as 13 percent annually—according to
H. B. Lary.[9] Lary and other writers[10] attribute this, at least in part,
to a faster rate of growth of world demand for manufactured goods
than for primary commodities. This can be documented by the 1963-68
growth rates of world exports: 29 percent for primary products and
75 percent for manufactures.[11] The phenomenon is understandable
in terms of the growing use of synthetic basic materials (e.g., plastics)
and economization in inputs of primary products (e.g., tin) per unit of
final output of manufactured goods.[12]

Exports of the developing countries are importantly affected by
the propensity of Americans to buy their products. The United States
is the world's largest import market. According to U.N. statistics,
the $26.8 billion of U.S. imports in 1967 constituted just under 12 per-
cent of the world's total imports. West Germany ranked a poor second
to this figure, with imports of only $17.4 billion.[13]

U.S. IMPORTS FROM THE
DEVELOPING COUNTRIES

To ascertain the nature of U.S. imports from selected developing
countries—hereafter referred to as SDCs—statistics were assembled
for the period 1964-70.[14] The countries chosen were drawn from the
"developing" category previously referred to and thus excluded the
major industrialized nations, such as Canada and Japan, as well as
all of Europe, and the developed non-European countries of South
Africa, Australia, and New Zealand. As a way of minimizing trade

patterns that might be warped by strong dependency relationships with industrialized countries or by the small size of the trade, only independent countries (U.N. members and countries associated with the United Nations) were selected (thus omitting Hong Kong); of these, only countries from which the United States imported a total of at least $10 million in 1968 were used.

The 54 countries selected had estimated per capita gross national products (GNPs) in 1967 ranging from $55 to $3,490 per annum, but the latter figure was for the small oil-rich country of Kuwait. All but 9 of the countries had per capita GNP's below $500 per annum; 9, under $100; 22, under $200; 33, under $300; and 40, under $400. Those with over $500 GNP were Panama ($550), Trinidad and Tobago ($790), Venezuela ($880), Uruguay ($550), Argentina ($800), Lebanon ($520), and Israel ($1,220). In three of these instances—Venezuela, Libya, and Kuwait—oil was the primary cause of the high per capita GNP level. For contrast, the corresponding figure for the United States was $3,670, and the range of the European Economic Community countries was $1,120 to $2,000 per annum.[15]

Table 1 presents the 54 SDCs, together with U.S. imports from each in 1964 and 1970. The $5.8 billion in imports in 1964 constituted 31 percent of total U.S. imports; the $8.6 billion in 1970 imports constituted less than 22 percent of total U.S. imports. On an aggregate basis, the value of imports from the SDCs increased 49 percent between 1964 and 1970. For the 54 nations, the median increase was 37 percent. All but 15 nations had increases, with rates ranging from 2 to 1,112 percent. Decreases ranged from 3 to 77 percent. In contrast, while aggregate imports from the SDCs increased 49 percent, total U.S. imports were increasing 115 percent, or more than twice as rapidly.

Ranking the SDCs in order of the value of imports they originated in 1964 (as shown in Table 1), the top third (18 countries) provided a considerably smaller proportion of total U.S. imports from the SDCs in 1970. Their 1964 share was 80 percent of total imports from the SDCs; in 1970 this had dropped to 71 percent. The next 18 SDCs increased their share from 15 percent in 1964 to 24 percent in 1968. The 18 SDCs supplying the smallest imports in 1964—5 percent of the total—continued to supply this proportion of the total in 1970.

Table 2 presents the size of import growth from the SDCs on a regional basis. Nine of the 11 North and Central American countries surpassed the SDC median growth of 37 percent, but only 4 of the 11 South American countries did so. Seven of the 15 Asian countries

TABLE 1

Seluted developing countries

U.S. Imports from SDCs, 1964 and 1970
(ranked in order of value of imports in 1964)

Country of Origin	U.S. Imports, 1964 ($ million)	U.S. Imports, 1970 ($ million)	Increase or Decrease, 1970 over 1964 (percent)
Venezuela	957.5	1,082.1	13
Mexico	607.3	1,222.4	101
Brazil	534.9	669.4	25
Philippines	396.5	475.9	20
India	309.7	298.1	-4
Colombia	278.7	268.9	-3
Chile	222.3	154.0	-31
Peru	196.6	340.5	73
Indonesia	166.9	182.2	9
Singapore and Malaysia	159.2	351.3	121
Dominican Republic	124.4	183.9	48
Trinidad and Tobago	116.3	235.6	103
Jamaica	115.5	185.9	61
Argentina	110.2	171.8	56
Ecuador	87.0	108.7	25
Saudi Arabia	85.9	19.7	-77
Ghana	77.8	90.7	17
Iran	77.5	66.8	-14
Taiwan	76.6	549.4	618
Ivory Coast	64.0	92.2	44
Guatemala	62.7	87.1	39
Israel	55.4	149.6	170
Costa Rica	54.0	116.4	116
Ethiopia	53.2	67.3	27
Kuwait	51.7	25.4	-51
Congo (Kinshasa)	48.8	40.6	-17
Liberia	48.4	50.9	5
Uganda	46.4	47.5	2
El Salvador	43.2	48.3	12
Honduras	41.0	102.4	150
Panama	40.1	75.5	88
Pakistan	39.5	80.2	103
Ceylon	36.1	26.4	-27

Country of Origin	U.S. Imports, 1964 ($ million)	U.S. Imports, 1970 ($ million)	Increase or Decrease, 1970 over 1964 (percent)
Nigeria	35.2	71.3	103
Nicaragua	33.6	61.4	83
Republic of Korea	30.5	370.2	1,112
Bolivia	28.7	24.8	-14
Libya	28.6	39.1	37
Thailand	24.7	100.0	306
Kenya	24.4	22.8	-6
United Arab Republic	24.3	22.9	-6
Burundi and Rwanda	24.2	21.2	-12
Haiti	24.1	31.9	32
Guyana	21.0	43.2	106
Malagasy Republic	18.2	31.7	74
Tanzania	14.0	23.8	70
Uruguay	12.8	19.2	50
Paraguay	11.0	10.6	-3
Federal Republic Cameroon	10.6	25.3	138
Afghanistan	10.3	3.9	-62
Lebanon	8.2	12.8	56
Central African Republic	7.3	6.4	-12
Gabon	7.1	8.9	26
Morocco	7.0	9.6	36
Total	5,791.3	8,627.4	49

Source: Based on data from U.S., Bureau of the Census, U.S. Imports of Merchandise for Consumption, Report FT 125, December, 1964 (Washington, D.C.: U.S. Government Printing Office, April, 1965); and U.S., Bureau of the Census, U.S. General Imports, Report FT 155, 1970 Annual (Washington, D.C.: U.S. Government Printing Office, 1971).

TABLE 2

U.S. Imports from SDCs, by Region
(ranked in order of size of increase, 1964-70)

Country of Origin	Increase or Decrease in U.S. Imports, 1970, Compared with 1964 (percent)
North and Central America	
Honduras	150
Costa Rica	116
Trinidad and Tobago	103
Mexico	101
Panama	88
Nicaragua	83
Jamaica	61
Dominican Republic	48
Guatemala	39
Haiti	32
El Salvador	12
South America	
Guyana	106
Peru	73
Argentina	56
Uruguay	50
Brazil	25
Ecuador	25
Venezuela	13
Colombia	-3
Paraguay	-3
Bolivia	-14
Chile	-31
Asia	
Republic of Korea	1,112
Taiwan	618
Thailand	306
Israel	170
Singapore and Malaysia	121
Pakistan	103
Lebanon	56

22

Country of Origin	Increase or Decrease in U.S. Imports, 1970, Compared with 1964 (percent)
Philippines	20
Indonesia	9
India	-4
Iran	-14
Ceylon	-27
Kuwait	-51
Afghanistan	-62
Saudi Arabia	-77
Africa	
Federal Republic Cameroon	138
Nigeria	103
Malagasy Republic	74
Tanzania	70
Ivory Coast	44
Libya	37
Morocco	36
Ethiopia	27
Gabon	26
Ghana	17
Liberia	5
Uganda	2
Kenya	-6
United Arab Republic	-6
Burundi and Rwanda	-12
Central African Republic	-12
Congo (Kinshasa)	-17

Source: Based on data from U.S., Bureau of the Census, U.S. Imports of Merchandise for Consumption, Report FT 125, December, 1964 (Washington, D.C.: U.S. Government Printing Office, April, 1965); and U.S., Bureau of the Census, U.S. General Imports, Report FT 155, 1970 Annual (Washington, D.C.: U.S. Government Printing Office, 1971).

surpassed the median, as did 6 of the 17 African countries. The biggest Western Hemisphere increase—Honduras—was only 150 percent, however, and other countries ranged down to a 31 percent drop for Chile. By contrast, 4 Asian countries—Korea (1,112), Taiwan (618), Thailand (306), and Israel (170)—had considerably higher increases. Decreases ranged down to 77 percent in Asia (Saudi Arabia) and to 17 percent in Africa (Congo).

Separately identified on Table 3 are 7 countries, the imports from which in 1970 were one half or more of Section 3 products— mineral fuels and lubricants. Imports from 4 of these countries increased, while 3 decreased, with the rates ranging from a 103 percent increase (Trinidad and Tobago) to a 77 percent decrease (Saudi Arabia).

Manufactured Imports from the SDCs

Table 4 presents the composition of U.S. imports from the SDCs in broad commodity groupings. Using a simple measure to distinguish relatively processed ("manufactured") from relatively unprocessed ("primary") products, SITC Sections 5 through 8—chemicals, manufactured goods classified chiefly by material, machinery and transportation equipment, and manufactured articles not elsewhere classified— accounted for an aggregate of 17 percent of total imports from the SDCs in 1964.* In 1970, this proportion had increased to almost 30 percent.

The picture that emerges from these tables is that over-all imports from the SDCs have been increasing, but the composition of such imports has been changing significantly. While imports of all commodity types—SITC sections 1 through 8—increased, the manufactured sectors increased much more rapidly than the primary-product sectors. Chemicals increased from 1.4 percent of imports from the SDCs to 1.8 percent; manufactured goods classified chiefly by material increased from 14 to 15 percent; machinery and transportation equipment rose from only 0.1 to 4.5 percent, the most rapid rate of increase; and miscellaneous manufactured articles grew from 1.5 to 8.6 percent

———————————

*As employed in the GATT statistics. Products in SITC sections 5-8 are hereafter referred to as "manufactured," but their degree of processing varies greatly, and processed products are found in other sections, as will be subsequently discussed with respect to SITC section 0.

TABLE 3

SDCs from Which Half or More of U.S. Imports
Were of Section 3 Products, 1970
(mineral fuels, lubricants, and related materials)

Country of Origin	Percent of Section 3 Products in U.S. Imports
Libya	94
Venezuela	84
Trinidad and Tobago	84
Kuwait	84
Saudi Arabia[a]	75
United Arab Republic	65
Nigeria	52

[a]Approximately 17 percent of imports were not classified by kind.

Source: Based on data from U.S., Bureau of the Census, U.S. General Imports, Report FT 155, 1970 Annual (Washington, D.C.: U.S. Government Printing Office, 1971).

the largest dollar increase. The 1970 manufactured component of imports from the SDCs of 30 percent still is, however, quite minor in comparison with the 65 percent that such products constituted in total U.S. imports that year.

Table 5 gives the proportion that SITC Sections 5 through 8 comprised of U.S. imports from each of the SDCs in 1970 and the change that this represented compared with 1964 (in percentage points). Of the 54 countries, 33, or over 60 percent, increased their section 5-8 proportions from 1 to 56 percentage points; 9 registered no change (7 of these were responsible for less than 1 percent of such imports in both years); and the remaining 12 showed declines ranging from 1 to 22 percentage points. The general upward movement of SITC sections 5-8 as a proportion of total imports from the SDCs is shown in that in 1964 less than 5 percent of U.S. imports from 25 of the countries were manufactured, whereas, in 1970 the number of such countries dropped to 23. In contrast, the number from which U.S. imports were 25 to 90 percent manufactured increased from 10 to 17.

TABLE 4

Proportions of U.S. Imports From SDCs, by
Type of Product, 1964 and 1970

SITC Section	Product Type	1964 Percent	1970 Percent
0	Food and live animals	40.9	37.7
1	Beverages and tobacco	0.5	0.5
2	Inedible crude materials excluding fuels	16.9	12.0
3	Mineral fuels and lubricants	22.0	16.5
4	Oils and fats, animal and vegetable	1.4	1.4
5	Chemicals	1.4	1.8
6	Manufactured goods classified chiefly by material	14.0	15.0
7	Machinery and transport equipment	0.1	4.5
8	Miscellaneous manufactured articles	1.5	8.6
	Total, sections 5 through 8	17.0	29.9
9	Not classified by kind	1.3	2.0
	Total	100.0	100.0

Source: Based on data from U.S., Bureau of the Census, U.S.
Imports of Merchandise for Consumption, Report FT 125, December,
1964 (Washington, D.C.: U.S. Government Printing Office, April, 1965);
and U.S., Bureau of the Census, U.S. General Imports, Report FT 155,
1970 Annual (Washington, D.C.: U.S. Government Printing Office,
1971).

On an area basis, the manufactured component of U.S. imports
increased from 7 of the 11 North and Central American SDCs (over
60 percent), from 10 of 15 of the Asian countries, and from 7 of the
11 South American countries. But from only 9 of the 17 African SDCs—
just over half—did the manufactured component of U.S. imports increase.
The lag of the African countries is partially understandable given that
less than 1 percent of U.S. imports from many of these countries are
manufactured goods.

Chemical Imports from the SDCs

Table 6 shows 1970 U.S. imports of SITC section 5 products (chemicals) from the 14 SDCs that provided $1 million or more of such products in that year. The proportions of imports under each category within this group are contrasted with the proportions of over-all U.S. chemical imports. All but 3 of the SDCs furnished imports in category 55, essential oils and perfume materials and toilet, polishing, and cleansing preparations; in 5 instances products under this category accounted for between 56 per'cent and 100 percent of total chemical imports. Only 6 percent of total U.S. chemical imports were in this category. The SDCs were also frequently represented in categories 51 (chemical elements and compounds), 54 (medicinal and pharmaceutical products), 56 (manufactured fertilizers and fertilizer materials), and 59 (chemical products and materials not elsewhere specified).

In summary, although section 5 is a relatively unimportant category for imports from the SDCs (1.8 percent of U.S. imports from SDCs versus 3.6 percent of total U.S. imports) and there appears to be a fair degree of diversity in the composition of such imports, some evidence exists of a concentration of trade in the relatively unprocessed categories.

Imports of Manufactures Classified by
Material from the SDCs

Table 7 examines the nature of the imports of SITC section 6 products (manufactured goods classified mainly by material), by far the most important manufactured-goods category of imports from the SDCs. The 15 SDCs from which the United States imported $10 million or more of such products in 1970 are shown on the table in rank order.

It will be noted from the table that for many of these countries, one or perhaps two of these categories accounted for well over 90 percent of the Group 6 imports they supplied. Of those listed, only Argentina, Brazil, and Mexico had less than 75 percent of their section 6 exports accounted for by categories 63-68. In the case of Brazil and Mexico, the addition of the iron and steel category (67) would bring the included total to 75 percent or more of their section 6 exports and would raise the Argentine total to over 40 percent. Iron and steel

TABLE 5

Proportion of Manufactured Products in
U.S. Imports from SDCs, 1970, and
Percentage Point Change from 1964

Country of Origin	Manufactured Products as Percent of 1970 Imports	Percentage Point Change from 1964
Republic of Korea	96	+30
Central African Republic	92	+17
Taiwan	89	+31
Israel	89	-4
Pakistan	81	+37
Chile	76	-8
Thailand	63	+56
India	62	+2
Singapore and Malaysia	54	+4
Peru	47	+14
Haiti	45	+26
Congo (Kinshasa)	44	+18
Uruguay	38	+23
Jamaica	36	+25
Mexico	32	+11
Argentina	27	+7
Morocco	27	+19
United Arab Republic	21	+4
Philippines	17	-2
Lebanon	16	-12
Afghanistan	14	+13
Iran	13	+3
Paraguay	12	-8
Brazil	10	+8
Tanzania	10	+6
Colombia	9	+6
Trinidad and Tobago	9	+2
Guyana	9	+1
Malagasy Republic	8	-1
Ceylon	6	+3
Kenya	5	+3
Indonesia	4	+2
Liberia	4	+2

Country of Origin	Manufactured Products as Percent of 1970 Imports	Percentage Point Change from 1964
Costa Rica	3	+2
Nigeria	3	-14
Federal Republic Cameroon	3	-13
Bolivia	3	-19
Honduras	2	+2
Guatemala	2	0
Panama	2	0
El Salvador	2	+2
Venezuela	1	+1
Ecuador	1	-1
Ivory Coast	1	+1
Ethiopia	1	+1
Dominican Republic	a	-3
Ghana	a	0
Nicaragua	a	0
Uganda	a	0
Libya	a	0
Kuwait	a	0
Burundi and Rwanda	a	0
Saudi Arabia	a	0
Gabon	a	-22

aLess than 0.5 percent.

Source: Based on data from U.S., Bureau of the Census, U.S. Imports of Merchandise for Consumption, Report FT 125, December, 1964 (Washington, D.C.: U.S. Government Printing Office, April, 1965); and U.S., Bureau of the Census, U.S. General Imports, Report FT 155, 1970 Annual (Washington, D.C.: U.S. Government Printing Office, 1971).

TABLE 6

SDCs from Which U.S. Imported $1 Million or More of Chemicals, by Category, 1970

Country of Origin	Section 5 Imports (thousand dollars)	Proportion by category[a] (thousand dollars)								
		51	52	53	54	55	56	57	58	59
Jamaica	56,289	99	—	—	—	1	—	—	—	—
Mexico	24,904	52	—	—	19	15	8	1	—	5
Trinidad and Tobago	16,557	75	—	—	—	—	23	—	—	2
Brazil	8,893	60	—	4	2	22	4	1	—	7
Argentina	7,425	12	—	35	5	10	—	—	—	38
Taiwan	6,857	22	—	—	—	35	—	21	22	—
Chile	4,771	55	—	—	—	—	45	—	—	—
Israel	4,688	18	—	—	29	2	44	—	7	—
India	2,950	17	—	2	12	61	—	2	—	6
Haiti	2,482	—	—	—	—	100	—	—	—	—
Malagasy Republic	2,413	—	—	—	—	100	—	—	—	—
Guyana	2,379	100	—	—	—	—	—	—	—	—
Indonesia	2,213	—	—	—	7	92	—	1	—	—
Paraguay	1,116	—	—	44	—	56	—	—	—	—
U.S. Total (million dollars)	1,450	52	1	6	6	6	13	2	8	6

[a]Category titles:
51 Chemical elements and compounds
52 Mineral, tar, tar oils, crude chemicals
53 Dyeing, tanning, coloring materials—natural and synthetic
54 Medicinal and pharmaceutical products
55 Essential oils, toilet, polishing, and cleansing preparations
56 Fertilizer materials
57 Explosives and pyrotechnics
58 Synthetic resins, regenerated cellulose, plastic products
59 Chemicals not elsewhere specified

Source: Based on data from U.S., Bureau of the Census, U.S. General Import. Report FT 155, 1970 Annual (Washington, D.C.: U.S. Government Printing Office, 1971).

TABLE 7

SDCs from Which U.S. Imported $10 Million or
More of SITC Section 6 Goods, 1970, Total
and by Selected Category[a]

| Country of Origin | Total | Section 6 Imports (million dollars) | | | | Selected Categories as Percent of Section 6 Total |
		Category 63	Category 65	Category 66	Category 68	
India	170	1	137	9	b	89
Peru	161	1	1	b	158	99
Singapore and Malaysia	132	10	3	b	119	100
Mexico	120	18	18	12	29	64
Chile	112	b	b	b	112	100
Republic of Korea	100	75	14	b	b	89
Israel	88	b	10	70	1	92
Taiwan	82	46	12	5	b	77
Thailand	62	1	b	3	58	100
Pakistan	61	b	60	b	b	99
Philippines	39	34	4	b	b	97
Brazil	37	5	13	5	2	67
Argentina	30	b	b	b	b	2
Colombia	21	2	4	8	33	82
Congo (Kinshasa)	17	1	b	b	16	100
Total U.S. imports	8,437	414	1,135	960	1,653	49

[a]Category titles:
    63 Wood and cork manufactures not elsewhere specified
    65 Textile yarn, fabrics, made-up articles, and related products
    66 Nonmetallic mineral manufactures not elsewhere specified
    68 Nonferrous metals
[b]Less than $500,000.

Source: Based on data from U.S., Bureau of the Census, U.S. General Imports, Report FT 155, 1970 Annual (Washington, D.C.: U.S. Government Printing Office, 1971).

imports into the United States on a massive scale are a relatively new phenomenon,[16] with Europe and Japan supplying by far the largest part of the total; however, Argentina, Brazil, and Mexican exports to the United States grew from $20 million in 1964 to over $40 million in 1970.

Machinery and Transport Equipment Imports from the SDCs

SITC section 7 (machinery and transportation equipment) is a relatively small export category for the SDCs, accounting for about 4.5 percent of 1970 U.S. imports from SDCs, as opposed to only 0.1 percent in 1964. Table 8 gives details on imports from the eight countries from which the United States purchased $1 million or more of section 7 goods in 1970.

Category 72 (electrical machinery and appliances) accounted for over 90 percent of U.S. section 7 imports from three of the leading suppliers, compared with only 20 percent of over-all U.S. imports. Most of the suppliers, nonetheless, were significantly represented in category 71 (nonelectrical machinery). Small proportions of the imports of all eight countries were in category 73, an important one in over all U.S. imports because it includes foreign-made automobiles.

Miscellaneous Manufactured Imports from the SDCs

SITC section 8 (miscellaneous manufactured articles) shows the varying degree of product concentration by the SDCs. As shown on Table 9, categories 84 (clothing) and 85 (footwear) comprised more than 75 percent of the total 1970 U.S. section 8 imports from the Philippines, Israel, Jamaica, Singapore-Malaysia, Trinidad-Tobago, and Costa Rica. The corresponding ratio for these categories in U.S. total imports of section 8 was 39 percent.

The last column on the table shows imports ranging from under $1 million to $92 million in category 89, (other miscellaneous manufactured articles). A wide range of articles were imported from the SDCs in this category, including miscellaneous articles of rubber and plastic, Christmas decorations, toys, sporting goods, works of art and antiques, wigs, brooms and brushes, umbrellas, phonograph records, and books and periodicals.

TABLE 8

SDCs from Which U.S. Imported $1 Million or
More of SITC Section 7 Goods, 1970,
Total and by Category[a]

Country of Origin	Section 7 Imports (million dollars)				Category 72 as Percent of Total
	Total	Cate-gory 71	Cate-gory 72	Cate-gory 73	
Mexico	154	34	107	13	70
Taiwan	141	7	128	6	91
Singapore and Malaysia	38	2	35	1	92
Republic of Korea	31	b	30	b	98
Argentina	8	7	b	b	1
Israel	8	4	4	b	43
Brazil	6	5	1	b	16
Jamaica	1	1	b	b	12
Total U.S. imports	11,200	3,000	2,300	5,900	20

[a]Category titles:
    71 Machinery, except electrical
    72 Electrical machinery and appliances
    73 Transportation equipment
[b]Less than $500,000.

Source: Based on data from U.S., Bureau of the Census, U.S.
General Imports, Report FT 155, 1970 Annual (Washington, D.C.:
U.S. Government Printing Office, 1971).

Processed Food Imports from the SDCs

As a further check on the degree to which the United States
imports processed products from the SDCs, an investigation was
made of certain categories in section 0 (food and live animals). The
nineteen SDCs that were the principal 1970 suppliers of products in
this section were selected for additional tabulation. The following
categories were reviewed: 1 (meat and meat preparations), 2 (dairy

TABLE 9

SDCs from Which U.S. Imported $2 Million or
More of Section 8 Goods, in 1970,
and Distribution by Selected Category

	Section 8 Imports (million dollars)				
Country of Origin	Total	Category 84 (clothing)	Category 85 (footwear)	Category 89 (other miscella- neous manu- factured articles)	Categories 84 & 85 as Percent Total
Republic of Korea	226	118	13	92	58
Taiwan	256	148	40	52	74
Mexico	99	28	85	49	38
Philippines	43	38	1	3	91
Israel	33	25	1	5	76
Jamaica	9	7	a	1	87
Singapore and Malaysia	19	15	a	4	78
India	11	3	3	3	60
Haiti	8	2	2	4	46
Trinidad and Tobago	4	3	—	b	88
Pakistan	4	2	a	1	43
Costa Rica	3	3	—	b	98
Argentina	2	1	a	1	38
Colombia	2	1	a	1	53
Total U.S. imports	4,844	1,267	629	1,910	39

aLess than $500,000.
bLess than 0.5 percent.

Source: Based on data from U.S., Bureau of the Census, U.S. General Imports, Report FT 155, 1970 Annual (Washington, D.C.: U.S. Government Printing Office, 1971).

products and eggs), 3 (fish and fish preparations), and 9 (miscellaneous food preparations). These four categories account for a relatively high degree of U.S. imports of processed foods. Meats involve slaughtering and chilling, or canning, operations; dairy products and eggs require processing, elaborate handling, or both; and about one fourth of U.S. imports of fish are preserved by relatively elaborate methods. Category 9 covers a variety of prepared food items.

The SDCs supplied relatively large amounts of meat and meat products (mostly from western hemisphere countries), little in the way of dairy products or eggs, substantial amounts of fish and fish products, and a small amount of miscellaneous food products. Table 10 gives the amounts of these imports from the countries listed in 1970.

There is some evidence that the proportion of processed foods in the imports of food products from the SDCs is gradually increasing. In 1964, the products studies ranged, as a percent of total imports of section 0 products from individual SDCs, from less than 1 percent to 71 percent (Argentina), with a median value of 5 percent. In 1970, they ranged from less than 1 percent to 82 percent (Argentina), with a median value of 9 percent. Between 1964 and 1970, imports of these products as a percent of total imports of section 0 products increased for sixteen of the nineteen countries, decreased for one, and stayed approximately the same for the remaining two.

RELATIONSHIP BETWEEN MANUFACTURED
SDC EXPORTS AND TOTAL SDC EXPORTS

Table 11 lists the 18 SDCs from which U.S. imports (in percent) have increased most rapidly between 1964 and 1970 and compares them with the 18 SDCs from which imports have shifted most rapidly into processed products (in percentage points of total imports). Some positive link between rate of increase of total imports and rate of increase of processed imports is shown by the appearance of 8 of the 18 countries in both columns of Table 11 and by the relatively high rank of Thailand, the Republic of Korea, and Taiwan in both columns. The link is not strong, however, since, presumably, 6 countries may have been expected to appear in both columns purely by chance. Accordingly, it is reasonable to conclude that the demand for manufactured exports is still only one of the several important factors determining the rate of growth of U.S. imports from a developing country.

TABLE 10

U.S. Imports of Processed Foods from SDCs, 1970

Country of Origin	Total	SITC Section 0 Imports[a] (million dollars)				Total of Categories 1-4 as Percent of Total for Section 0
		Category 01	Category 02	Category 03	Category 04	
Mexico	573.7	42.9	b	83.1	0.3	22
Guatemala	80.1	13.7	b	2.8	b	21
Honduras	85.1	10.5	b	4.9	b	18
Nicaragua	51.6	25.4	b	6.7	b	62
Costa Rica	111.1	18.8	b	3.3	b	20
Dominican Republic	159.3	3.7	b	0.2	b	2
Panama	59.2	2.4	b	13.9	b	28
Colombia	198.7	b	b	5.2	b	3
Ecuador	101.6	b	b	8.9	b	9
Peru	117.9	b	b	5.4	b	5
Brazil	516.0	15.9	0.5	16.3	b	6
Argentina	97.2	74.1	1.4	4.2	0.7	82
India	82.3	2.8	b	18.8	0.1	26
Indonesia	56.2	0.3	b	0.2	b	9
Philippines	230.2	b	b	0.7	b	c
Taiwan	51.1	b	0.2	6.2	0.1	13
Ivory Coast	89.1	b	b	3.9	b	4
Ghana	85.5	b	b	0.4	b	1
Ethiopia	64.6	b	b	*	b	c

[a]Category titles:
  01 Meat and meat preparations
  02 Dairy products and eggs
  03 Fish and fish preparations
  04 Miscellaneous food preparations

[b]Less than $50,000.

[c]Less than 0.5 percent.

Source: Based on data from U.S., Bureau of the Census, U.S. General Imports, Report FT 155, 1970 Annual (Washington, D.C.: U.S. Government Printing Office, 1971).

TABLE 11

SDCs from Which Imports and Manufactured Imports
Grew Most Rapidly, 1964-70

Country of Origin	Increase of U.S. Imports, 1970 over 1964 Percent	Country of Origin	Increase in Proportion of Manu- factured Goods Percentage points
Republic of Korea	1,112	Thailand	56
Taiwan	618	Pakistan	37
Thailand	306	Taiwan	31
Israel	170	Republic of Korea	30
Honduras	150	Haiti	26
Federal Republic Cameroon	138	Jamaica	25
Singapore and Malaysia	121	Uruguay	23
Costa Rica	116	Morocco	19
Guyana	106	Congo (Kinshasa)	18
Trinidad and Tobago	103	Central African Republic	17
Pakistan	103	Peru	14
Nigeria	103	Afghanistan	13
Mexico	101	Mexico	11
Panama	88	Brazil	8
Nicaragua	83	Argentina	7
Malagasy Republic	74	Tanzania	6
Peru	73	Colombia	6
Tanzania	70	Singapore and Malaysia	4

Source: Based on data from U.S., Bureau of the Census, U.S. Imports of Merchandise for Consumption, Report FT 125, December, 1964, (Washington, D.C.: U.S. Government Printing Office, April, 1965); and U.S. Bureau of the Census, U.S. General Imports, Report FT 155, 1970 Annual (Washington, D.C.: U.S. Government Printing Office, 1971).

SUMMARY

United States imports from developing countries (represented by the SDC group chosen for analysis) have been increasing. During the period 1964-70, in current prices, they rose 49 percent in the aggregate. Imports from 39 of the 54 countries increased, rates of increase for individual countries ranging from 2 to 1,112 percent.

Notwithstanding this general picture of growth, imports from the developing countries have grown less rapidly than over-all U.S. imports. Total U.S. imports increased 115 percent between 1964 and 1970. As a result, imports from the developing countries dropped from 31 percent of total U.S. imports in 1964 to under 22 percent in 1970.

The composition of imports from the developing countries has been changing. The more highly processed products of sections 5 through 8 comprised only 17 percent of U.S. imports from the developing countries in 1964, but over 28 percent of such imports in 1970.[17] There is also evidence that imports of processed food products have also been increasing.

There were concentrations in most of the processed-products imports in a few types of commodities, however, notably textiles and clothing, processed metals and minerals, a limited range of wood products, and footwear, as well as in certain other types of labor-intensive products.[18] Some of these products are subject to the kind of drawbacks related to primary commodities with respect to price elasticity or the processing may be minimal, thus contributing little to the build-up of industrialization in the originating countries. Others, such as textiles and footwear, face a restrictive outlook in the United States, as well as in other developed-country markets, because their rate of growth has been so rapid that domestic industries have mounted strong campaigns looking toward quantitative controls. Such controls, at the moment of writing, already apply to cotton products* and may eventually be applied to noncotton textile products as well.

---

*The Long-Term Arrangement on Cotton Textiles, originally negotiated in Geneva in 1962.

NOTES

1. General Agreement of Tariffs and Trade (GATT), Inter-national Trade 1968 (Geneva: Secretariat of the Contracting Parties, 1969), p. 1.

2. Ibid. Because of a drop in export unit values, the volume increase was 12 percent, "a post-war, and possibly an all-time record."

3. GATT, International Trade 1969 (Geneva: Secretariat of the Contracting Parties, 1970), p. 1.

4. International Trade 1968, Table 31, pp. 114-15, supplemented by GATT, International Trade 1967, (Geneva: Secretariat of the Contracting Parties, 1968), Table 17, pp. 80-81. "Developing countries" are defined as those of Latin America, Asia (except Japan), the Middle East, and Africa (except South Africa). Australia and New Zealand are excluded. International Trade 1968, pp. 293-94.

5. As a matter of fact, exports of such products from developing countries have been increasing at a faster rate than world exports of such products. International Trade 1968, p. 3.

6. SITC sections 5 through 8. Ibid., pp. 295-96.

7. Ibid., Table 31.

8. B. A. DeVries, The Export Experience of Developing Countries, International Bank for Reconstruction and Development Occasional Paper No. 3 (Baltimore, Md.: Johns Hopkins Press, 1967), Ch. 2.

9. H. B. Lary, Imports of Manufactures from Less Developed Countries (New York: National Bureau of Economic Research, 1968), p. 109.

10. "Other writers" are B. Balassa and United Nations Statistical Office Publications.

11. International Trade 1968, Table 31, supplemented by International Trade 1967, Table 17.

12. Alfred Maizels, Industrial Growth and World Trade (London: Cambridge University Press, 1963), p. 84.

13. United Nations Yearbook of International Statistics, 1967 (New York, 1969), Table A, pp. 12-15.

14. The statistics that follow, and those in the tables, were secured from the following publications: U.S., Bureau of the Census, U.S. Imports of Merchandise for Consumption, Report FT 125, December, 1964 (Washington, D.C.: U.S. Government Printing Office, April, 1965); and U.S., Bureau of the Census, U.S. General Imports, Report FT 155, 1970 Annual (Washington, D.C.: U.S. Government Printing Office, 1971).

The change in the published figures from "imports for consumption" to "general imports" (which includes imports brought into bonded warehouses) creates some degree of possible error in the 1964-70 comparisons. According to the Census Bureau, however, "consumption" and "general" data are almost identical when annual figures are used.

15. World Bank Atlas (Washington, D.C.: International Bank for Reconstruction and Development, 1969).

16. Thus, U.S. steel imports grew from 2.7 million net tons in 1960 (6 percent of world imports) to 10.8 million net tons in 1966 (17 percent of world imports). Approximately 90 percent of the imports in 1966 came from Europe and Japan. U.S., Congress, Senate, Committee on Finance, Steel Imports, S. Rept., 90th Cong., 1st Sess. (Washington, D.C.: U.S. Government Printing Office, 1967), Table A-11, p. 265, and Table D-6, p. 339.

17. The Commission on International Development States that "the feature of the recent trade experience of developing countries which holds out the greatest promise for the future was the extraordinary growth in exports of manufactured goods." Commission for the International Bank for Reconstruction and Development, Partners in Development (New York: Praeger, 1969), p. 87.

18. A similar conclusion concerning manufactured exports of the developing countries appears in International Trade 1968, p. 8: "While gradually diversifying, exports of manufactured products from developing countries remain heavily concentrated on a few product groups—namely, nonferrous metals, textiles and miscellaneous (mainly light) manufactures. . . . The note on Exports of Engineering Products from Selected Industrializing Countries, . . . shows that what sustained progress there has been in such exports towards industrial areas has occured in a rather narrow category of products (mainly radio receivers, tape recorders, television sets and other electrical household appliances, as well as electronic components)."

An analysis of relative shares of the U.S. import market shows that between 1962 and 1968 some of the developing countries have actually been displacing Japan as a source of some of the types of manufactured imports mentioned. <u>International Trade 1968</u>, Table E, p. 304.

CHAPTER

3

DEMAND

FACTORS

FOR

MANUFACTURED

IMPORTS

PRICE VERSUS NONPRICE DEMAND FACTORS

The purpose of this chapter is to examine the demand influences affecting imports of manufactured products from the developing countries and to explore the manner in which these influences may promote the expansion of such imports. Demand influences may be broadly characterized as price and nonprice. Price influences on demand can be demonstrated in terms of a conventional demand-curve representation. The concept of increasing demand for a given product by reducing its price—quantitatively defined as the "elasticity of demand"— has been amply documented in economic literature.[1] Nonprice influences on demand may be much more subtle, and they form the basis for much of current marketing theory. As will be indicated in this chapter, such demand influences are of particular importance when trade moves from primary products to manufactured products, because product differentiation becomes a much more common occurrence.

Nonprice influences on demand are also of special importance because price reductions—other than those implied by tariff reductions—presumably would require the achievement of lower cost levels by suppliers of manufactured products in the developing countries. But such an achievement is likely only from a change in technology, which is excluded from consideration here (see Chapter 1), or from the economies of increased volume, which might have to wait indefinitely until other influences increase demand.

This chapter first takes up the issue of product differentiation, and its importance in considering manufactured imports from the

developing countries. Following this, tariffs as a demand influence
are considered, in the light of (a) current proposals for the reduction
or removal of tariffs in favor of imports from the developing countries,
and (b) the August, 1971, U.S. import surcharge. It will be seen that,
while tariffs are presumably a price influence on demand, the response
to tariff changes may actually be largely in nonprice terms. Finally,
the chapter deals with other nonprice influences on demand, including
the exporter-importer relationship and marketing know-how.

MANUFACTURED IMPORTS AND PRODUCT DIFFERENTIATION

It is possible to generalize broadly that primary products are
usually homogeneous in nature and manufactured products are not.
The homogeneity of primary products is in part due to their nature—
for example, mineral ores found even in different parts of the world
may have many properties in common—but it is also largely due to
conscious efforts that have been made over the years to establish
nationally and internationally recognized standards for homogeneity.
Thus, the U.S. Department of Agriculture can report on such crop
categories as "middling white upland cotton, 1-1/16 inch staple
length" or "sorghum grain, No. 2 yellow."

There are, of course, important exceptions to this general rule
of manufactured-good differentiation. Under the influence largely of
informed bodies of users, certain products, particularly those that
serve as capital-goods inputs (e.g., steel and cement) are produced
to specified standards. But most other manufactured capital goods
and consumer goods, other than certain processed foods, are related
to one another only in that they perform the same general function.
Thus, there are U.S. government-established standards for beef and
canned fruit;[2] but packaged puddings, canned soups, chairs, cutlery,
air conditioners, and bicycles are all, to a greater or lesser extent,
the unique creations of their producers. The transition of developing
countries from primary-product exports to exports of manufactured
products is accordingly largely a transition from undifferentiated
products to differentiated products.

Product differentiation has, of course, been a key factor in the
supplanting of "perfect competition" in price theory with the theories
of "imperfect" or "monopolistic" competition.[3] While the monopolistic
element of such theories may seem to rest heavily on the name and
advertised reputation of a particular manufacturer, even unadvertised
imports from suppliers without established trademarks can exhibit

nonprice competitive strengths. It is clear that trademarks like Kodak and Coca Cola lift their makers well above direct price competition with lesser-known producers of equivalent products. But the differentiation factor of manufactured goods need not be associated with a trademark. A filing cabinet that looks like an end table or a garden tool with a beautifully carved teak handle has a market characteristic that combats straight price competition just as does a product with a well-known trademark.

The supplier of a manufactured import from the developing country faces an entirely different selling situation than the supplier of a primary product. He has typically moved out of a market characterized by the horizontal demand curve—a market where limitless quantities of his homogeneous product can be taken at the market price—to a situation represented by a sloping demand curve. But more important, because of the potential for differentiating his product, this demand curve may be largely manipulatable. Rather than simply being able to sell different quantities at different prices, the seller, by changing the nature of the product he offers, can move the demand curve.[4] For example, improving a manufactured product can shift its entire demand curve to the right, resulting in a greater number of units demanded at any one time at a number of different prices. Moving to the opposite extreme, a product lacking necessary characteristics may suffer from zero demand at various prices. An electrical appliance designed for the American market but wired for 220 rather than 110 volts could represent the latter situation.

Without denying the basic economic truths of the theory of comparative cost, international trade in manufactured products takes on much more complex parameters when viewed in this light. It is presumably not possible economically to export umbrellas from Saudi Arabia, where all the materials and components must first be imported from other areas; but the availability of steel and cloth in India does not mean that a product with the quality, design, packaging, and other manufacturing attributes desired can reach the American market.[5]

THE ROLE OF TARIFFS

Just as comparative costs underlie the economics of international trade in manufactured goods, notwithstanding the questions of manufactured-product differentiation, so tariffs have an important role in such trade. It would seem inescapable, for example, that the preferential rates granted by Canada to British imports enabled such imports to hold a more substantial share of the Canadian market against imports from the U.S. than they would have otherwise, in view of the strong freight-cost advantage of the imports from the United States.[6] On the other hand, it must be similarly clear that Germany's overwhelming share of the American market for imported cars cannot be explained by tariffs, since British, French, and Italian cars are subject to identical rates of duty.

In any event, a careful examination of the role of U.S. tariffs as an impediment to manufactured imports from the developing countries is justified, at minimum, by the efforts of such countries to eliminate these tariffs on a preferential basis. Until August, 1971, developing countries presumably viewed U.S. tariffs only as targets for potential reduction in their favor. Then suddenly, on the evening of August 15, a new element entered the picture—the 10 percent surcharge on U.S. imports adopted in connection with the dollar crisis. Accordingly, the discussion that follows treats both the potential effects of U.S. tariff reductions in favor of the developing countries and the potential effect of U.S. tariff increases such as the (hopefully temporary) surcharge.

"Tariff preferences" for the developing countries have been a major issue in international-trade discussions among nations since the 1964 Geneva meeting of the United Nations Conference on Trade and Development (UNCTAD). Preferential schemes in general involve the removal or reduction of tariffs by the industrialized countries in favor of the developing countries. Tariffs between the industrialized countries would not be affected; this is the "preferential" nature of the proposals.[7]

The European Economic Community (EEC) has already instituted a system of preferential tariff reductions in favor of developing countries. On July 1, 1971, the EEC put into effect reduced tariffs on about 150 processed agricultural products and established duty-free quotas on manufactured products based on the amount imported from the developing countries in 1968, plus 5 percent of the imports of each type of product in the preceding year from the industrialized countries. Beneficiaries of the tariff preferences are the countries comprising the "Group of 77" of UNCTAD, increased, since its formation, to a total of 91 countries.[8]

At the time of writing, the future of U.S. tariff preferences is clouded by the dollar crisis and the import surcharge. But it remains likely that the administration will eventually present to Congress some type of tariff-preference proposal to implement promises made by the United States at several international conferences. Developing countries have asked for the preferential removal of the import surcharge, but this request has been refused.

Clearly, preferential access to the U.S. market will benefit exporters of manufactured products from the developing countries. Quantification of this benefit is difficult to project, because the exact correlation between tariff reductions and trade increases is a next-to-impossible analytical task.[9] Nonetheless, some clue to the possible benefit of tariff preferences can be gained by reviewing the height of the U.S. tariffs to be reduced or removed.

An analysis of the U.S. tariff rates in effect prior to the 1967 conclusion of the Kennedy Round of tariff negotiations on items of interest to the developing countries in connection with their export-expansion goals indicated that over one third of the rates were 10 percent ad valorem or less, two thirds were 20 percent ad valorem or less, and only one out of twenty-five was over 50 percent ad valorem.[10] It has been estimated that the Kennedy Round reduced these particular rates in the U.S. tariff schedules by either 32 or 35 percent, depending upon the weighting used.[11] If a reduction of one third is taken as an example, as of the final effective date of the U.S. Kennedy Round tariff reductions (January 1, 1972) one third of the rates will be less than 7 percent ad valorem, two thirds of the rates will be less than 14 percent ad valorem, and five sixths will be 20 percent ad valorem or less.

The potential reduction in the landed cost of an import stemming from elimination of, let us say, a 15 percent tariff, can be estimated in the following way:

Price of the import, f.o.b. country of origin	$100
Freight and insurance	$ 10
U.S. tariff on f.o.b. value	$ 15
Total landed cost before removal of tariff	$125
Landed cost after removal of tariff	$110
Percent reduction	12%

The fact that most of the potential reductions in landed cost will be well under 12 percent is perhaps a sobering thought to exporters or potential exporters in the developing countries, who have tended to place great reliance in the stimulative effects of preferential tariff reductions.

Some attention must now be given to the question of "effective" rates of tariff protection. In recent years, tariff researchers have subjected rates to a new type of analysis that purportedly shows that, even while "nominal" (published) rates may be moderate, "effective" rates can have a highly protective effect in excluding exports or potential exports from developing countries.[12] Effective rates are based on the difference between the importing country's tariff on a raw or unprocessed product and its tariff on the processed or manufactured product made from it. They are tabulated in the value added in the exporting country. As an example, if a mineral ore is permitted duty-free entry into the United States but is dutied at 10 percent ad valorem in its refined state and if refining adds only 10 percent to its value, then the effective rate would be considered 100 percent rather than the nominal 10 percent.

Effective-rate analysis adds an important dimension to tariff studies. It focuses on the relationship of one tariff rate to another, emphasizing that an importing country may attempt to sequester the processing function to itself by establishing high tariffs on finished products and low (or duty-free) rates on raw inputs. This historically has been largely true in the United States, except in the case of temperate agricultural products, where tariffs or other trade restrictions are typically highly restrictive on imports.

A practical demonstration of the effective-tariff argument was probably the action taken by the United States in removing the tariff against processed coffee. Green coffee has traditionally been duty free. After the repeal of the tariff on processed coffee, a highly successful instant-coffee-manufacturing industry developed in Brazil. The success of this enterprise was so great, as a matter of fact, that exports of Brazilian instant coffee were the subject of critical negotiations between the United States and Brazil in connection with the renewal of the International Coffee Agreement.[13]

The coffee example may be used to illustrate a limitation in the effective-rate approach. It applies very well in the case of processed or manufactured products whose major or even overwhelming cost component is a primary product not produced in the importing country. Instant coffee meets this requirement, but a doll would not. A doll, like many other manufactured products, generally represents a composite of many materials (plastic, rubber, glass and other mineral products, metal, textiles) and may include subassemblies purchased by the manufacturer from other suppliers in his country or abroad. In such a case, other complex comparative cost relationships are apt to be more important than the effective rate of tariff protection, if, indeed, one could be calculated for a product such as this. Further-more, the level of effective rates depends on the relationship of raw-material and end-product tariffs; as end-product tariffs come down progressively, the base on which such effective rates are calculated may become too small to support much of a protective effect.

To sum up the tariff-reduction question, it should not be argued that U.S. tariffs are without protective effect, particularly when viewed in the case of individual items for which nominal rates are high and other processed items for which effective rates are substantial. Any hope that the widespread reduction of tariff rates, as in connection with a preference scheme, will automatically promote enormous in-creases in trade, however, should be subject to much closer scrutiny.

Turning now to the question of the manner in which a tariff reduction, such as that resulting from the proposed tariff preferences, would affect the volume of imports of manufactured products from the developing countries, the question arises as to whether this effect would manifest itself mainly through price competition or whether nonprice competition would be involved. Appendix B presents an analysis of the possible effect of tariff preferences on the position of all sellers in the American market, using conventional classical competitive assumptions. In brief, the lowering of the costs of a group of sellers would be presumed to affect the over-all supply schedule in the market, resulting in a lower market price and a greater repre-sentation of the benefited sellers in the market.

That a tariff reduction should promote the expansion of imports from the developing countries need not be challenged. What should be questioned, however, is whether this expansion will take place pri-marily through price reductions. Most sellers of manufactured goods, because their products are not homogeneous, can and will compete in all respects except price reductions whenever possible. Direct price reductions all too often must be countered by competitors, and sellers tend to feel that the resulting lower price level can be harmful to all suppliers, because demand elasticity may be insufficient to maintain what they consider to be adequate profit levels. Instead, competition among sellers of manufactured goods is more apt to be in terms of, or at least to include, the various nonprice marketing accommodations, ranging from quasi-price actions, such as quantity-per-dollar increase, to such indirect accommodations as better credit terms.

Following through the cost reduction implied by a lowered tariff to its likely impact upon sales of an import from a developing country, one concludes that, unless the supplier raises his price by an equivalent amount, the tariff cost saving will mean a reduction in landed cost to the importer. The latter may choose not to lower his price to his customers, in which case his margin (the difference between cost and selling price) will be increased. But this increased margin can be put into sales promotional activities ranging from additional personal selling to advertising. Or an indirect price reduction can be offered by providing additional accommodations to the customer ranging from a willingness to accept small-quantity orders to extra-cost delivery services for greater promptness.

All or part of the cost reduction can alternatively be passed on to customers who may not choose to give this directly to those to whom they sell. Nonetheless, they may take actions that increase sales because of the additional margin that they thereby earn. For example, a supermarket operator knows that certain display positions or even certain amounts or types of shelf position can sell more merchandise because the product meets the shopper's eye more directly and because the positions favor comfortable self-service selection.[14] He cannot give these superior positions to all his merchandise, but a more favorable profit margin may induce him to give one to the import on which he has been given a cost reduction.

Turning back to the supplier in the developing country, what alternatives has he when given the opportunity to supply a product more cheaply to his importer in the United States? He may choose to "capture" all or part of the potential saving by investing more in his production or handling of the product. As will be discussed in detail in the ensuing chapters, there are a number of marketing accommodations that can have a profound effect on the demand for the imported product, ranging from a more appropriate design to a better package. It should be borne in mind that actions of the type just referred to are as genuinely competitive as price reductions (or the implied price reduction to the importer resulting from holding the price unchanged in the face of the tariff elimination).

In terms of Appendix Figure 1, these actions can be visualized as factors to move the demand curve to the right. To reconstruct the actual form of typical competition, improved marketing accommodations add utility to the product and therefore create a whole new demand schedule for it, with increased quantities taken at any given price level. This is a more realistic model of how the market for manufactured products is likely to work. The principal types of such accommodations will be examined in greater detail in subsequent chapters.

The preceding discussion may now be reversed to consider the possible effect of tariff increases, such as that involved in the August, 1971, U.S. import surcharge. On the basis of the figures cited earlier, one can reason that the typical increases in landed cost resulting from the surcharge will be in the 7 to 9 percent range. In highly price-competitive lines, such increases may be critical to the volume of trade. But the preceding discussion should have demonstrated that the marketing of manufactured products involves a variety of competitive techniques other than price. As evidence of this, suppliers of certain types of manufactured goods predicted, after the imposition of the surcharge, that their exports to the United States would not be reduced. Not to be discounted, even by the developing countries, is the import-curtailing potential of the de facto devaluation resulting from the floating of the dollar that also began in August, 1971. Nonetheless, the arsenal of marketing techniques available to cope with any such price effects will doubtlessly be used by suppliers of manufactured products from the industrialized countries; they should be similarly available to suppliers or potential suppliers from the developing countries.

THE IMPORTER-EXPORTER RELATIONSHIP*

The preceding discussion has in effect concentrated on an explanation of international trading by examining the factors that go into an individual transaction. The discussion was still couched essentially in terms of what might take place when a group of buyers and sellers with little or no knowledge of one another gathered together physically in an auction-type situation and made exchanges based on the most advantageous terms, as cited on the spot. The mere statement of these assumptions suggests that this is not the way buyers and sellers operate in a typical international trading situation, particularly when manufactured goods are involved.

The numerous marketing accommodations that a buyer requires of a seller—for example, product specifications, quality, promptness, packing, documentation—mean that a satisfactory trading relationship is potentially one of the most valuable assets an importer can have. Therefore, the relationship between importer and exporter must usually be the result of a detailed, diligent search by the importer

---

*Henceforth, the discussion will refer to importers according to the letter code in Appendix A—e.g., AA, AB, AC, etc.

leading to a careful choice of exporter. This produces two somewhat contradictory tendencies in importer operations: an inertia against changing from an established source of supply and a ceaseless concern about finding new suppliers that will meet the standards of the importer.* New suppliers are desired for business expansion, for replacement of currently unsatisfactory suppliers, or as a hedge against possible future problems with current suppliers.[15]

As will be discussed in detail in Chapter 7, importers may be broadly classified into different categories: specialists, who sell a limited number of lines to wholesalers or other resellers, and mass merchandisers, such as department-store and mail-order buying chains, which are integrated right through to the final purchaser. The specialist-importer is likely to make the search for new suppliers a highly individualized quest, involving travel to the country and detailed negotiations with new potential sources by one of the principals of the firm. The importing firm may be inundated with unsolicited offers to sell from overseas but may still discard all such proposals in favor of the personalized source selection (importers BM and BT). The mass-merchandising importer, on the other hand, may have an elaborate set of buying offices overseas whose duty it is to locate potential sources of supply and make preliminary determinations of their adequacy prior to the visit by buying officials from the U.S. company. The latter conclude the pricing and delivery details, leaving local buying-office staff to follow through on fulfillment.

In general, the relationship of a U.S. importer with a new source of supply may be traced as follows: location of the supplier, securing product samples, placing initial orders, and placing volume follow-up orders.** A reasonable economic interpretation of the source-selection process might be to amortize the initial location costs over,

---

*Importers AY, BF, BH, BT, CD, and CS specifically referred to the need for constant travel to develop and maintain sources of supply. Sometimes, as in the case of importer BD, sources are quite difficult to locate (musical instruments). This frequently may be a factor in instances where importers express a satisfaction with current sources. Importer BT states that, in view of the number of years it has taken to develop satisfactory sources, his firm "will remain with our present suppliers until they have priced themselves out of the market, and we will cross that bridge when we come to it."

**Importers AW, AY, BF, BT, and CB point to the difficulties, the risks, and the expense of developing new sources, especially in

say, the initial two-year purchasing period.* These costs, incidentally, must be applied against those sources that are selected, meaning that each selection bears the overhead of those selection efforts that failed. In addition, during the early period of relationship with this new source, a series of misadventures may occur, such as late delivery, substandard quality, inadequate packing, misinterpreted specifications, and so on. Any one of these could, of course, be fatal to the buyer-seller relation-ship, if the importer concludes that the error is not correctable. At minimum, however, they must be charged as "start-up" costs of the new supply source.

Figure 1 attempts to visualize the cost and margin relationships between an importer and a new source of supply during an initial five-year period. The figure shows that the desired margin is not achieved by the importer until the third year of the relationship. The gross margin is practically nil on early orders, while both error costs are being absorbed, and the cost of locating the new source is being amortized. As stated, the latter is amortized in two years; the former is presumed, in the figure, to last for more than two years. Because, in this example, the difference between buying price and selling price is greater than the gross margin that the importer hopes to net, it can be seen that by the end of the third year he is netting more than his target margin. But if the relationship does not last long enough, he fails to achieve his target margin level.

In sum, the importer's ability to earn the gross margins, and accordingly the profits, necessary to sustain his operation must be visualized over a period of time, rather than in terms of an individual transaction, particularly in the case of manufactured goods.

---

countries from which the importer has not previously purchased. Importer BH (mass merchandiser) has products of neighboring countries grouped at his overseas buying centers to minimize the travel of his buying staff. Importer CB states that the price offered by a new source must be sufficiently lower to cover the initial costs of perfecting the new buying relationship.

*The period chosen is arbitrary. The writer has the impression that exporter-importer relationships of five to ten years may be typical, but no data were gathered on this point.

FIGURE 1

Cost and Margin Relationships
Between Importer and New Source of Supply[a]

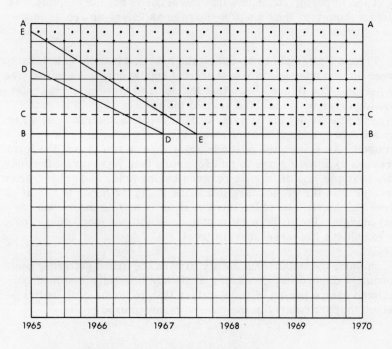

Line A-A represents importer's selling price
Line B-B represents importer's cost of product
Line C-C represents importer's target average cost
Area DBD represents importer's cost of locating
    new source, amortized over two years
Area EDDE represents cost of initial errors by exporter
Area AEEBA represents importer's gross margin over
    five year period

[a]A constant rate of transactions over time is assumed.

MARKETING KNOWLEDGE AS A LIMITING
FACTOR IN TYPES OF MANUFACTURED IMPORTS

In Chapter 1, it was pointed out that developing countries have certain limitations on their ability to export manufactured products. Chief among these are shortages of capital and know-how. H. B. Lary, in Imports of Manufacturers from the Less-Developed Countries, discusses the extent to which capital shortages have favored the development of labor-intensive export industries in many of these countries. He believes that additional growth is likely to take place in this type of trade. Chapter 2 has indicated the extreme concentration of imports from the developing countries on certain types of products, such as textiles. Although, in the aggregate, a fair variety of manufactured goods are imported from the developing countries, most of these countries have successfully developed only a few types of manufactured products that are exported to the United States.

A further diversification of manufactured imports from the developing countries would not simply provide new horizons for the over-all increase of manufactured imports from the developing countries. It would also reduce the economic impact of such imports in the United States by distributing them more broadly across industry lines. This should decrease the likelihood of protectionist reactions from domestic producers. Textiles and shoes, it has already been announced, are to be exempted from any preferential tariff reduction scheme proposed by the U.S. government, presumably because of such reactions.

Consideration of the multiplicity and complexity of marketing factors that have been mentioned in this chapter suggests that the shortage of know-how by exporters and potential exporters in the developing countries may be as much, and in many instances more, on the marketing than on the production side. Yet, marketing knowledge may be easier and less expensive to come by. U.S. importing organizations, striving to secure and maintain adequate supply sources, are doubtlessly particularly willing to help. Their need is primarily for interested and receptive producers and exporters in the developing countries.

The time may be especially propitious. Western Europe and Japan, the traditional suppliers of U.S. manufactured imports, have been enjoying periods of unprecedented prosperity and growth. In some instances, importers report that their previous suppliers no longer can or will give the time and attention to sale and delivery that they formerly did.* The need and the opportunity appear to exist; it remains to be seen whether they can be brought together.

SUMMARY

In this chapter, demand influences on imports of manufactured products from the developing countries have been separated into price and nonprice factors. The special importance of nonprice competition has been emphasized, particularly because of the product differentiation that is characteristic of most types of manufactured goods.

The role of U.S. tariffs as a demand-influencing factor was next examined. It was found that the height of most such tariffs at present is not such as to inspire reliance upon their reduction or removal as a way of achieving the rate of import expansion that developing countries may desire; that tariff reductions may be employed for nonprice competition, rather than for what the classical economic approach might suggest in the way of price competition; and that it may be possible to counter tariff increases, by the same token, by using offsetting marketing accommodations.

International trade was then examined in terms of the relationship, preferably long-standing, between importers and their suppliers, rather than as a series of individual transactions. The complexities of such relationships and the cost of establishing new ones was analyzed as a guide to trade expansion.

Finally, it was indicated that the concentration of imports of manufactured goods from the developing countries in limited-product categories may be explainable in large part not by capital or production know-how shortages, but rather by the lack of marketing know-how. The incentive to correct this situation may be particularly strong because of the decreasing interest in the American market evidenced by certain traditional suppliers of manufactured imports.

---

*Importer AB refers to the diminution of quality and care in orders filled by his Japanese suppliers and to more stringent minimum-order requirements. Importer BG states that the move to new sources of supply in recent years parallels the growth of German exports in previous years, when importers felt that their English suppliers were not interested in the needs of their customers.

NOTES

1. An overview of competitive price theory is presented in George Stigler, The Theory of Competitive Price (New York: Macmillan, 1942).

2. According to the Fruit and Vegetable Division of the U.S. Department of Agriculture's Consumer and Marketing Service, there were over 150 U.S. standards for grades of processed fruits, vegetables, and related products as of July 20, 1970. See also U.S., Department of Agriculture, Official U.S. Standards for Grades of Carcass Beef (Washington, D.C.: Department of Agriculture Consumer and Marketing Service S.R.A. 99, June, 1965), reprint of 1926 issue.

3. The two most important works revising competitive theory are: Joan Robinson, Economics of Imperfect Competition (London: Macmillan, 1934); and Edward Chamberlin, Theory of Monopolistic Competition (2d ed.; Cambridge, Mass.: Harvard University Press, 1936). For a contemporary view, see Donald Dewey, The Theory of Imperfect Competition: A Radical Reconstruction (New York: Columbia University Press, 1969).

4. In many American consumer markets, price does assert itself as a competitive benchmark, but not in the classical competitive sense. Custom has frequently ordained that many products will be offered in retail outlets at "price points": that is, men's bathing suits may be priced at $4.95 and $9.95, women's purses at $8.50 and $12.50, or infants' blankets at $3 and $6. In each case, the store's buyer has in mind a consumer image of a proper price to pay for a type of merchandise, and he selects, from what his suppliers offer him, products to stock for that image. See J. W. Wingate and E. O. Schaller, Techniques of Retail Merchandising (Englewood Cliffs, N.J.: Prentice-Hall, 1956), pp. 162-64.

But an examination of the products offered may reveal greater diversity than similarity within each price point. One bathing suit has a lining, the other a patented belt; one purse has a distinctive plastic insert, another an inner compartment; one blanket is made of a superior synthetic fabric, the other has a satin binding. In other words, diversity prevails again, although some limitations have been established: the supplier who proposes to sell a product that would retail (on the basis of accepted trade margins) between or above established retail price points may find no buyers. In some cases, however, the distinctiveness of a manufacturer's product (i.e., his competitive monopoly, in theoretical terms) may enable him to sell in accordance with a pricing formula he has established for himself.

5. The American view is exemplified by this comment about U.S. exports: "Our most successful exporters invariably meet price competition overseas by dramatizing the additional benefits their products offer and thus convince the prospective end-user that they offer greater value. It can be done. It has been done. And it continues to be done in every country, every day. This is being demonstrated by innumerable case histories in nearly every field of industry." C. J. Olson and R. C. Ellis, Export or Die (Chicago: Dartnell, 1966), p. 58.

6. See U.S., Department of Commerce, Bureau of International Commerce, Basic Data on the Economy of Canada, OBR 67-98 (Washington, D.C.: U.S. Government Printing Office, December 1967), p. 23.

7. Such preferences would be global in nature rather than the present limited political preferences, such as those between the EEC and certain African countries. One of the most detailed studies of this subject is Sidney Weintraub, Trade Preferences for Less-Developed Countries (New York: Praeger, 1966).

8. The EEC and Generalized Preferences, Information Memo P-17 (Brussels: Commission of the European Communities, June, 1971).

9. See, for example, L. B. Krause, "United States Imports and the Tariff," American Economic Review, May, 1959, pp. 542-51; and M. Kreinin, "Effect of Tariff Changes on the Prices and Volumes of Imports," American Economic Review, June, 1961, pp. 310-24.

10. A. H. Small, "Expansion of Manufactured Imports from the Less-Developed Countries Considered in the Light of Proposals for Tariff Preferences," Law and Policy in International Business, Winter, 1969, p. 113.

11. Ernest Preeg, Traders and Diplomats (Washington, D.C.: The Brookings Institution, 1970), p. 230.

12. The landmark paper on this subject was probably Bela Ballassa, Tariff Protection in Industrial Countries: An Evaluation," Journal of Political Economy, December, 1965, pp. 573-94.

13. "The Brazilian Soluble Coffee Problem," Quarterly Review of Economics and Business, Spring, 1969, pp. 29-38.

14. E. A. Brand, Modern Supermarket Operation (New York: Fairchild Publications, 1963), p. 76.

15. The development of import contacts for Korean products through a campaign to induce mass-merchandising buyers to go to that country is described in Amicus Most, Expanding Imports: A Case Study of the Korean Experience (Washington, D.C.: U.S. Agency for International Development, 1969), pp. 118-20.

4

THE DESIGN IS THE PRODUCT

To a large extent, the design is the product in the American market today. To justify the preceding statement, a distinction needs to be drawn between alternative meanings of the word "design." Design is sometimes thought of as the external features of an object, such as the classical facade placed on an otherwise conventional modern building. Design, however, can be conceived of as the very creation of the object. In this view, it is the designer who selects certain basic materials and prescribes their transformation into a product that is wanted for a particular use. In the broadest sense, designing a product can be considered to be recognizing the need for it.[1] This is the sense of design employed in this chapter.

The definition can be illustrated as follows. An American automobile manufacturer decides that he wants to reach the tremendous American market for a very compact, simple, easy-to-maintain, car, which is presently being served by the Volkswagen and similar imported cars. He makes certain basic decisions on size, components, materials, and operating characteristics and thereby creates a product (such as GM's Vega or Ford's Pinto). Although at some stage in the planning of this new automobile, sculptor-engineers contour the hood, fenders, roof-line, etc., this is mere "styling." The design really was embodied in the initial decisions in the front office.[2]

The example may be overdrawn because many products are chiefly purchased for their external features, such as decorative textiles or paintings. But design should be considered the concept of the product, rather than the details of its finishing. Design is not limited to shape and surface, but encompasses the purpose of the

maker in offering it to the market (to what use is it to be put?) and
therefore includes materials, capacities, durability, versatility, and
so forth.[3]

It is obvious that an economic product—i.e., one that can be sold
in the market—must represent the answer to an end-user's need. Stated
in this way, the needs of the market place might seem to be stable requirements for such necessities as food, shelter and clothing. And
stated in this way, the definition would therefore bypass the most
dynamic, the most rapidly growing, and the most promising aspect
of the American market—the fact that most purchasing is discretionary,
i.e., the specific purchase involves a wide range of options.[4]

In optional purchasing, the need has probably been strongly influenced by the seller. The American public accepts as part of its
humorous folklore that such things as halitosis and "tired blood" did
not exist until they were created by advertisers—and yet these phrases
have been used in selling millions of dollars worth of mouthwash and
patent medicines.[5] Even business purchasing is not immune from
inspired wants. "Prestige" office furniture is frequently advertised
in the same publications and in the same manner as high-priced home
furniture. At the same time, designers of products have increasingly
been freeing themselves from established ways of doing things, and
from established materials, offering new approaches to the satisfaction
of traditional wants. The American homeowner needs a seat for his
recreation room; suppliers have met this need by fabricating vinyl
plastic film into an inflatable couch. Products designed to meet traditional or induced needs may resemble nothing ever seen before in
the American market such as a box, advertised as a "toy for the
executive," that flashes colored lights in meaningless random succession or a camel saddle, used not for riding across the desert, but as
a low stool to be placed in the living room.

Tables 12 and 13 are designed to illustrate the degree to which
U.S. per capita purchases differ from those of other countries in
variety (the number of options) as well as in quantity. The tables
permit a contrast between the international range of per capita consumption of foodstuffs with that of newsprint. As shown in Table 12,
the daily number of calories consumed in the country with the highest
per capita food consumption is about twice that of the country with the
lowest consumption. Table 13, however, shows that for newsprint—
a product that is utilized in a variety of optional uses ranging from
newspapers to packaging material—the ratio is greater than 40 to 1.
The average individual in the United States consumes about twice the
number of calories as the individual in the lowest-consumption country, but 40 times the quantity of newsprint.

TABLE 12

Food Consumption:
Calories per Day per Capita

Calories	Number of Countries
1,700 up to 1,800	1
1,800 up to 1,900	6
1,900 up to 2,000	7
2,000 up to 2,100	7
2,100 up to 2,200	10
2,200 up to 2,300	5
2,300 up to 2,400	5
2,400 up to 2,500	5
2,500 up to 2,600	4
2,600 up to 2,700	4
2,700 up to 2,800	1
2,800 up to 2,900	6
2,900 up to 3,000	8
3,000 up to 3,100	3
3,100 up to 3,200	9
3,200 up to 3,300	2
3,300 up to 3,400	1[a]
3,400 up to 3,500	1

[a]United States.

Source: United Nations, Yearbook of International Statistics, 1967 (New York, 1969), Table 159, pp. 478-82. The year used is 1966 or latest available.

TABLE 13

Newsprint Consumption:
Kilograms per Capita per Year

Kilograms	Number of Countries
Less than 1	25
1 up to 2	8
2 up to 3	12
3 up to 4	10
4 up to 5	4
5 up to 6	7
6 up to 7	1
7 up to 8	1
8 up to 9	1
9 up to 10	1
10 up to 11	1
11 up to 12	2
12 up to 13	3
13 up to 14	1
14 up to 15	0
15 up to 16	1
16 up to 17	2
17 up to 18	0
18 up to 19	1
19 up to 20	0
20 up to 21	0
21 up to 22	0
22 up to 23	0
23 up to 24	0
24 up to 25	3

TABLE 13 (Continued)

Kilograms	Number of Countries
25 up to 26	1
26 up to 27	0
27 up to 28	0
28 up to 29	0
29 up to 30	0
30 up to 31	1
31 up to 32	0
32 up to 33	0
33 up to 34	1
34 up to 35	0
35 up to 36	0
36 up to 37	1
37 up to 38	0
38 up to 39	0
39 up to 40	0
40 up to 41	0
41 up to 42	1[a]

[a]United States.

Source: United Nations, Yearbook of International Statistics, 1967 (New York, 1969), Table 171, pp. 500-501. Figures are for 1968.

    Another way of looking at the degree to which American con-
sumers have purchase options is through U.S. government studies
relating to poverty. In 1968, for example, less than 13 percent of
all Americans were adjudged to be on the poverty level; the figure
had declined more than 5 percent since 1959. The government's definition of poverty, expressed in simplified terms, is a family income
of less than three times the cost of a specified, modest food diet.[6]

Stated another way, in 1968, 7 out of every 8 Americans were spending less—usually considerably less—than one third of their income for food. This represents the culmination of a long process of real-income growth in the United States. Urban wage earners in 1875 were able to devote only 6 cents of each dollar they earned to nonnecessities; by 1950, this had risen to 43 cents.[7]

The monumental study Expenditure Patterns of the American Family found that the average American family in 1960-61 spent less than one quarter of its income for food, one fifth of which was for food prepared in restaurants; less than one quarter of its income for housing and housing operations, with actual shelter costs only about half of this amount; and just over 10 percent for clothing and accessories. The optionals included 15 percent for transportation, mostly invested in family automobiles; almost 7 percent for medical care; close to 3 percent for personal care; 4 percent for recreation and equipment; and about 2 percent for reading and education.[8]

Indeed, for most Americans, practically every purchase has a substantial degree of optionality to it. Although there are still many developing countries in which perhaps a dozen foodstuffs comprise almost the entire diet of the bulk of the population, Americans make daily choices between beef and lamb, between salad and cooked vegetables, between baked desserts and ice cream, and so forth. And even for the same food, the decision may rest between buying raw potatoes to be cooked at home, or canned potatoes to be served as potato salad, or frozen french-fried potatoes to be reheated. Or the entire main course may be purchased as a "TV dinner," so that home food preparation is at a minimum. Similarly, a major part of the American family's clothing budget does not go for a limited variety of standard garments, but for such optionalities as pants suits for women and hiking boots for men. Shelter purchases are apt to include such categories as camping trailers.

Obviously, the American market is not the only one that is characterized by a considerable degree of optionality. Even in developing countries, among segments of the population for whom nutritional sufficiency is a major problem, such options as soft drinks and snack foods may be widely purchased.[9] But it will not be until average incomes in such instances reach much higher levels that the American degree of purchase optionality can be achieved.

IMPULSE SALES:
PURCHASE OPTIONALITY ILLUSTRATED

The American tourist wandering through a foreign bazaar is an example of deliberately unplanned purchasing. Before he emerges, the tourist is likely to be the proud possessor of one or more objects for which a preknown need could not possibly have existed. Only by the merest coincidence are his purchases likely to minister to the satisfaction of basic necessities. At most, his acquisition may be to fulfill a need that he previously created for himself—e.g., some brassware or glass object to add to a hobby collection. American shoppers every day of the year wander through the aisles of grocery supermarkets, department stores, drug stores, and similar self-service outlets as through a bazaar; regularly bringing to the cashier at the checkout counter a variety of unplanned purchases for which little or no need was anticipated by the purchaser at the time he entered the store.

This American "impulse purchasing" is stimulated by all of the advertising media, ranging from newspapers to television and including mailings to the home. Sellers are thus continually evoking "needs" for such things as art courses and books with identical bindings.[10] The growth, volume and variety of impulse purchasing are impressive. A study by the DuPont Company, a major seller of transparent films, estimated that practically half of the purchases in supermarkets were completely unplanned; that is, the shopper entered the store without even a general idea of making half the purchases actually made.[11] Impulse purchasing is importantly affected by packaging, a subject dealt with in the Chapter 6. Suffice it to say here that this type of purchasing demonstrates the capabilities of the American market to absorb product creations on a scale that would never be anticipated in an economy where most buyers are severely restricted in their purchase choices by their limited disposable income.

THE RELATIONSHIP OF
DESIGN AND FUNCTION

Bearing in mind the previous discussion, it is obviously inappropriate to say that form follows function; the form may create the function or the function may disappear from American life because of changes in the purchaser's environment and later reemerge in a different way.

The clothespin serves as a humble but appropriate example. As a lathe-turned wood product, it probably was for many decades as dependable a part of the American scene as the horse and wagon. But just as newer forms and materials, such as plastics and steel springs, began to make their appearance in clothespins immediately after World War II, the wide advent of gas and electric clothes driers began to eliminate the clothespin entirely. The drier not only represented liberation for the American housewife from the hazards of weather, but, for families in skyscraper apartment houses, it provided a welcome answer to the loss of yard or roof space. No sooner had the clothespin staged its virtual disappearance from the American scene, however, than a new technology arrived—wash-and-wear clothing. For the first time, the wearer was able to doff garments worn during the day, rinse them, even in a motel room sink, and hang them over the tub to be ready for the following day. The new opportunity created a new need: a clothespin! Nothing like the old product, of course, but small and light, prepared so that a set of them could be sold with their own carrying case, to be dropped into the traveler's luggage.

Sometimes an opportunity for a new product need is created by a change in some other major product on the market. American automakers, during the 1950s, abandoned the use of dashboard gauges to indicate engine temperature and oil pressure, substituting warning lights in their place. Auto-accessory suppliers immediately began to offer clip-on gauges that the car owner could install himself. The evolution continues.

But even such conventional illustrations of form and function do not adequately reflect the optionality of purchases in the American market. A manual on product design, for example, says: "The table lamp you buy for a living room should not only look like a lamp and be appropriate to the surroundings in which you will place it, but it should also give the amount of general illumination you want and as much light as you need on the objects on your table, and at the same time not shine in anyone's eyes."[12] The appropriateness of the above is obvious, and nothing that is said here should in any way imply that there is not a market in the United States for such sensible and utilitarian lamps. A very successful recent development in the American home lighting field, however, consists of a large light bulb that is an aluminized decorative sphere when not lit and exposes a bare filament when lit. Such a product defies every precept of the preceding quotation. Yet, as a novel and attractive addition to many homes, it apparently has found wide acceptance.

In summary, the point may be made that after the American consumer has met the simple and obvious needs of his daily life, including the need for adequate home lighting, he is still free to indulge in many of his less rational desires for novelty and distinctiveness.

"NEW" PRODUCTS

The just-cited example is typical of a vital segment of the American market—the "new product." "New" has been said to be one of the most potent words in the American promotional vocabulary, although its use has been subject to some advertising exaggeration. Some products, for example, are claimed by their advertisers to be new even after decades of use—perhaps because there is constantly a new generation of teenagers, or homemakers, whatever the purchasing group, that has not been exposed to the advertising before.[13]

Some products are genuinely and completely new, such as ultra-sonic cleaning devices. The household purchaser of such a device never realized that he wanted to clean his old razor until presented with a device that could do the job. Other products perform functions in a completely new way, such as electronic desk calculators. Or some invent functions to be performed, such as the "executive toy" mentioned earlier in this chapter. Even the package may be the "newness" of the product, as in the case of the shoe polish container to be described in Chapter 6. A major change in consumer marketing occurred when producers of household detergents began to offer their products in sizes approximating those of suitcases.

So established has the new-product aspect of American marketing become that supermarket chains frequently have a permanent "buying committee" before whom vendor representatives make their appearance to argue in favor of a new offering. Successful aspirants have their product placed on the shelves for a given test period, during which careful calculations are made to determine whether the new product is as profitable to the store for the display space used as possible alternative products.

There are few rules to the new-product game, as played in the American market. Genuine product advantages, in a technical sense, are helpful, but not in and of themselves sufficient. Nonwoven fabrics, an excellent and low-cost wiping material, made several unsuccessful

debuts before they secured a regular place in the market. On the
other hand, it is perfectly possible that some seller may market a
toothbrush with a 12-inch handle, and, given the right combination of
imaginative promotional support, convince buyers that the product
has an important inherent advantage over regular toothbrush handles.
Unfortunately, as shall be discussed in the section on design mortality,
his monopoly might be short-lived.

It is particularly important to emphasize that the newness of a
product is only its newness to the American market or even its newness
to a particular segment of that market.[14] Staplers, for example, had
been used in American offices for many decades before marketers
began to produce simple and inexpensive models for home use. The
home stapler in marketing terms was as new a product as the stapler
when it was first introduced for office use. The antiquity of the Hindu
sitar does not diminish its newness to the American scene; few Americans had heard of it until an increasing interest in the culture of India
made it a popular musical instrument for concert and amateur use.

DESIGN MORTALITY

The selling opportunity for what is new and different in the
American market has its darker side: products can also suffer from
early market mortality. The American buyer's option of purchasing
a new product today frequently becomes his option of abandoning it
tomorrow in favor of some other new product.

There is doubtlessly a spectrum of product mortality for products
in the American market. Some, such as imported liqueurs, catering
to a select few, may be safe from loss of demand for many decades,
whereas, at the other extreme, children's toys and fads, such as hula
hoops, may be gone in a season.[15] Other products, such as the home
staplers previously mentioned, have a saturation factor that causes
demand for them to grow very rapidly in the early years after their
introduction, but then to taper sharply when the major part of the
initial demand has been met.

Fashion goods are the main type of product that comes to mind
when design mortality is mentioned. While fashion is involved, in a
sense, in all types of products ranging from phonograph records to
snack foods, most people think of fashion primarily in terms of clothing and such personal accessories as costume jewelry.[16] Foreign
suppliers are at a basic disadvantage when fashion is involved, since
they are geographically and culturally more isolated from the

American market than domestic producers. By coincidence, however, fashion goods are largely textile products, for which comparative cost elements favor the exporter in many countries, and the subcontracting approach to design is employed to bridge the supplier-to-market distance.

As developing country suppliers become more heavily involved in the American market, they are bound to feel more of the fashion burden in their marketing. In mid-1970, for example, New York's major department stores had widely varying forecasts of the preferences of women buyers with respect to skirt lengths. Some stores were placing their orders predominantly for "mini" lengths, others predominantly for "midi" or "maxi" lengths.[17] It can be seen that the difference in fashion expectations, although perhaps partly justified by the different types of clientele of these stores, was such as to impose a major hazard on suppliers, and this hazard was felt right in New York City, within a few blocks of the buying offices of the stores involved, by the clothing producers whose orders depend on the fashion trends.[18]

American buyers, however, will place firm orders, even if of more limited size than the supplier considers desirable, for fashion merchandise from abroad. The problem for many suppliers is to accomodate their production and shipment to the timing required for delivery of these products (the delivery-timing problem applies to all imports—see Chapter 8—but is continually important in fashion products). If a fashion-inspired Christmas accessory is desired for sale in a store in Pittsburgh, the importer will contract a certain number of months ahead, dependent on shipment to a particular port of entry within a certain time period before the holiday so that delivery to Pittsburgh can take place just at the time that the merchandise is required by buyers in the store in response to seasonally-placed advertising.[19] Early delivery of seasonal merchandise can mean excessive storage costs to the buyer. As for late delivery, there is nothing as unattractive to the merchandising manager of a retail store as Christmas products delivered on December 26.

THE DEGREE OF DESIGN DISTINCTIVENESS

The design of a product can be entirely unique or entirely imitative. Many gradations exist between these two extremes. It might be useful, nonetheless, to attempt a characterization of the degree of design uniqueness, or distinctiveness, by establishing the following three broad general design categories: distinctive-purpose designs, distinctive-image designs, and accepted-image designs.

Distinctive-purpose designs are those that cater to a user-want previously unidentified. Foreign-origin products of this nature have provided some of the most popular trends in the recent American market. The Finnish sauna, for example, catered to a health desire previously unknown to the general American market. The Japanese hibachi capitalized on an interest in charcoal cooking with a new device, heavier in its construction than the charcoal grill previously in use. The Mexican sarape inspired a new trend in American wearing apparel. Much more common, however, is the distinctive-image design, in which a traditional function, like that of a table knife, is performed by a product with an appearance other products do not have. Imported examples of distinctive-image designs include Swedish modern stainless-steel flatware and recent designs of Danish furniture. Oriental rugs are considered to be in this category. Most common are products of accepted-image design. Some are really imitations, such as fountains pens that are made like those of the Parker Pen Co.; others, like the antique-style telephones that have recently become a popular sale item, imitate a general type of design.

An importer succeeding in popularizing a distinctive-purpose design—in other words, in tapping a new outlet for American optional purchasing—may indeed have staged a marketing coup from which the supplying country can benefit handsomely (until the imitators arrive in force, at any rate). There may be many distinctive-purpose design products in the developing countries that will some day successfully ensconce themselves in the American market—products like the Philippine barong tagalog, an embroidered men's dress shirt. Similarly, wide opportunities still exist for distinctive-image designs. The current interest of black Americans in their cultural heritage, for example, has opened a market for African-inspired designs. But notwithstanding such possible important exceptions, the overwhelming bulk of the marketing opportunities are in accepted-image designs. The developing countries rarely have the good fortune to be the beneficiaries of new American design trends and are unlikely in the forseeable future to have the financial resources necessary themselves to promote such trends in the American market.

The foregoing discussion suggests that there may be considerable pressure on developing-country suppliers of manufactured products to conform to design trends already established in the American market. Importers are the point at which this pressure is exercised.[20] Sometimes the need for conformance is explicit:

Case History BR-1

The product was a soccer ball from India (importer BR). The department store chain retailing the ball found it satisfactory, except in one respect—the valve did not fit American hand pumps. The supplier was able to replace the valve with a compatible design on subsequent shipments.

At other times, a design divergence from a developing country may be modest enough to be acceptable in the American market.

Case History AB-1

A hunting rifle, made in South America, is probably not as conveniently designed as some of the competitive American products. It is so unusual in its appearance, however, that one importer (AB), as the exclusive American agent, has done a satisfactory volume of business with it.

As will be discussed in Chapter 7 different types of importers have different requirements in the matter of design distinctiveness. Specialist importers are frequently in the forefront of design trends and may be much more willing to accept designs as they find them in the exporting country, since their customers are frequently of the type that market products catering to the more adventurous final buyer, the consumer who prides himself on his willingness to adopt new things. Mass-merchandising importers, on the other hand, cater to the vast middle-majority American market, and their designs must be accordingly more eclectic, more established, and more middle of the road. All importers, however, are apt to make demands on their suppliers to adapt their products to the American market to some degree, and this is where a source of importer-exporter friction frequently arises. An American importer (CU) says, "they feel if it is acceptable in the home market, it is saleable in the United States." (This type of criticism will reappear in the discussion of product quality.)

The most extreme type of importing of accepted-image products may be said to be the use of subcontracting, in which the importer has a fixed image of what he wants—sometimes with exact blueprints and specifications—and orders the product produced for him abroad.

Case History BZ-1

Small, decorated baskets for children are almost as much
a part of the American scene at Easter as tree decorations
are at Christmas. Importer BZ had been receiving his
supply from Japan for many years, but lost his sources. A
representative of the Korean consulate, seeking business
from New York importers, was given a sample of the basket
and located a Korean supplier. Samples and subsequent
shipments were entirely satisfactory.

It is likely that there is a considerable amount of this type of
purchasing from the developing countries. Consider as circumstan-
tial evidence that developing countries are already supplying the
American market with products in such sophisticated categories as
microscopes (the Philippines), medical equipment (Pakistan), ortho-
pedic devices (Trinidad and Colombia), speed-measuring devices
(Mexico), and electrical instruments (Israel).[21]

Almost all purchasing of manufactured products from abroad
by American industrial firms is likely to represent subcontracting,
since these firms must establish exact requirements for products
that will serve as components in their end products. Some indication
of the size and growth of this manufactured-product importing may
be gained from recent statistics compiled by the U.S. Tariff Commission on imports under Section 807 of the U.S. Tariff Schedules. This
section provides duty exemption for the value of American-made components incorporated in products assembled abroad and shipped back
into the United States. By the nature of this trade, all products would
involve the subcontracting approach. Between 1966 and 1969, the
value of Section 807 imports rose from $890 million to $1.6 billion.
Some of the developing countries importantly identified with the imports were Mexico (originating $145 million of such imports in 1969),
Taiwan ($68 million), Korea ($20 million), and the Philippines ($5
million).[22]

SUMMARY

In this chapter, a distinction has been drawn between design in
the external sense and design as the very creation or conception of
a product. The importance of the latter concept has been emphasized
in marketing products to the American buyer.

The optionality of American purchases has been illustrated
both statistically in terms of the relatively small portion of the

American consumer's dollar that is devoted to items traditionally considered as the necessities, and qualitatively, in terms of the way in which a major portion of American purchases represent responses to wants created either through advertising, or through display at the point of purchase. Design accordingly may be viewed as a rapidly shifting service to the American market, capitalizing on current trends and opportunities to cater to wants that are very largely product-created.

The constant desire of American buyers for new products in turn threatens the mortality of products that have established themselves in the market; the foreign supplier needs the assistance of the importer in exact scheduling of deliveries to avoid the penalties of out-of-date, out-of-style production.

Designs of imports can be broadly characterized as distinctive-purpose, distinctive-image, and accepted-image in nature. Although distinctive-purpose designs from abroad have figured recently in American marketing trends and distinctive-image imports are even more common, most imports from the developing countries are in the accepted-image design category. Specialist importers are more likely to accept designs as they find them in the developing countries than mass-merchandising importers, but both may require exporters to make at least minor modifications in the design of their products, a fact that has been the source of difficulty in exporter-importer relations. Subcontracting—when the importer specifies exactly the product he wants—is an important type of accepted-image design importing, particularly in the industrial field.

NOTES

1. But the need can be fulfilled in a variety of ways previously undreamed of. A chair can be made by gluing pieces of wood together—the traditional way—or by spraying plastic on metal mesh. Don Wall Wallace, Shaping America's Products (New York: Reinhold, 1956), p. 1. Henry Dreyfuss, Designing for People (New York: Simon and Schuster, 1955), p. 18, refers to this as "design from the inside out, not from the outside in."

2. See "The Minis Meet the Imports," Business Week, August 15, 1970, pp. 68-71. The nature of the design function and how it is handled are discussed in the National Industrial Conference Board, Organization for New Product Development (New York, 1966).

3. The American motivation for "something better" is

exemplified in the following quotation: "The fact is that the value and cost of our products must be measured not by money alone but in the light of the fact that they can make lives either pleasant and full or dreary and meaningless. If we can acknowledge this, we have learned the real cost of ugliness." Nathan Cabot Hale, "The Value of Good Design," in The Case for Good Design (New York: American Management Association, 1963), p. 3.

4. Says Steuart Britt, in a book on American consumption patterms,"most consumer income goes for 'discretionary' purchases, for things we want but don't necessarily have . . . sometimes for products we didn't even dream of owning just a few years back." Steuart Britt, The Spenders (New York: McGraw-Hill, 1960), p. 74.

5. For an account of how American advertising "invented" the consumer's "wants," see James P. Wood, The Story of Advertising (New York: Ronald Press, 1958), pp. 384-85. For samples of advertising including "Blood Poverty" from the 1890s and early 1900s, see ibid., pp. 328-29.

6. U.S., Bureau of the Census, Current Population Reports, "Poverty in the United States: 1959 and 1968," Series P-60, No. 68, (Washington: U.S. Government Printing Office, 1969), pp. 1, 11.

7. U.S., Department of Labor, How American Buying Habits Change (Washington, D.C.: U.S. Government Printing Office, 1959), pp. 35-36.

8. Adapted from "Summary of Consumer Expenditures for Goods and Services," in National Industrial Conference Board, Expenditure Patterns of the American Family (New York, 1965), p. 16.

9. See U.S., Department of Commerce, Bureau of International Commerce, The Market for Food Processing and Packaging Machinery and Equipment in the Philippines, DIB 71-08-512 (Washington, D.C.: Commercial Intelligence Division, October, 1970).

10. See George Katona on "Artifically Created Wants" in George Katona et al., The Mass Consumption Society (New York: McGraw-Hill, 1964), pp. 54-61.

11. E. I. du Pont de Nemours and Company, Consumer Buying Habits Studies (Wilmington, Del., 1965). The attention attracted by this work causes Britt to refer to impulse buying as "DuPont's Law." Britt, The Spenders, p. 109. For a discussion of the marketing

implications of impulse buying see James Engel, David Kollat, and Roger Blackwell, Consumer Behavior (New York: Holt, Rinehart and Winston, 1968), pp. 497-99.

12. U.S., Small Business Administration, Design Is Your Business (Washington, D.C.: U.S. Government Printing Office, 1953), p. 19.

13. Marketers frequently try to find some of the advantages of newness for old products through fresh selling approaches. See Peter Hilton, Keeping Old Products New (Englewood Cliffs, N.J.: Prentice-Hall, 1967), pp. 35-36.

14. "The new-products race in industrial markets, though often less visible and carried out with less fanfare, is no less intense than that going on in consumer markets." Morgan MacDonald, Jr., Appraising the Market for New Industrial Products, Business Policy Study No. 123 (New York: National Industrial Conference Board, 1967), p. ii.

15. Fads have been characterized as "empty products," i.e., devoid of benefits other than novelty and attention. The reasoning is that this causes demand suddenly to collapse, rather than declining gradually. C. R. Wasson and D. H. McConaughy, Buying Behavior and Marketing Decisions (New York: Appleton-Century-Crofts, 1968), pp. 96-97.

16. "Fashion, in its most general sense, evidences itself not only in what people wear but in what they do, how they live, and the things they use." Jeanette Jarnow and Beatrice Judelle, Inside the Fashion Business (New York: John Wiley and Sons, 1965), p. 1.

17. New York Times, June 8, 1970, p. 46, col. 2.

18. Marketing analysts have attempted to describe the characteristics of fashion cycles, suggesting growth curve patterns, and the signals of approaching saturation and decline. See C. R. Wasson, "How Predictable Are Fashion and Other Product Life Cycles," and William H. Reynolds, "Cars and Clothing: Understanding Fashion Trends," Journal of Marketing, July, 1968, pp. 36-43 and 44-49, respectively. As noted above, however, the uncertainty with respect to women's clothing styles in 1970 caught even experienced American marketers in problems of unpredictable evolutions of consumer style demand.

19. Irving Goldenthal, How to Plan Stocks, Sales and Open-to-buy (Philadelphia: Chilton Co., 1953), pp. 18-19.

20. The problem of bridging the gap between craftsman-producer and foreign buyer in developing countries is discussed by James Warren in the International Trade Forum, December, 1966, pp. 20-22.

21. Countries are listed by name in Import tables of Schedule 7, in U.S., Tariff Commission, Summaries of Trade and Tariff Information, TC Publication 322, Vol. II (Washington, D.C., 1970).

22. U.S., Tariff Commission, Economic Factors Affecting the Use of Items 807.00 and 806.30 of the Tariff Schedules of the United States, Investigation 332-61 (Washington, D.C., September, 1970), pp. 37, 66.

CHAPTER

5

QUALITY

ISSUES

FOR THE

AMERICAN

MARKET

THE QUALITY CRISIS IN THE U.S. MARKET

In the preceding chapter, the importance of relating the design of a product to the purposes of the intended end-user was discussed. Adapting Webster's Third New International Dictionary definition of quality, one may say that the quality of a product is its degree of excellence in meeting these purposes.[1] The following discussion will bring out some of the complexities of both the achievement and the perception of quality.

Quality has almost become a "fighting word" to Americans because of their stated disillusionment, in recent years, with the products they purchase. The favorite target of consumers has been the American automobile. But the complaint that "nothing works any more" is leveled against all types of consumer products, nondurables coming in for their share of disparagement. And the consumer complaint is echoed by many businessmen, who either attribute their own quality problems to a lessened degree of quality in the components and materials that they buy or who maintain that the entire level of their operations has been adversely affected by the deterioration of quality levels.

To what extent is this presumed quality crisis real, and to what extent is it imagined? Statistical measures abound, but in the social sciences one rarely has laboratory conditions for validation of a hypothesis. Warranty claims, accident rates, average product life are all figures that apply only to a given year; it is impossible to say whether 1965 cars in the hands of 1970 drivers would have performed better.

There are two general types of comments made about current American product quality. Those who believe it has fallen point to the sustained period of American economic growth and relative full employment as a "relaxant" to American production personnel (both labor and management). Employees and businesses are no longer under the harsh competitive conditions of the depressed 1930s, according to this argument, but have literally grown up in a period of prolonged strong demand that helped even mediocre products survive in the U.S. market. In many production situations, it is said, unions could bargain for wage rates and work rules that made products increasingly expensive, and management could react by seeking progressively to lower the labor content per dollar of product, with quality again the potential victim.[2]

A response to this argument might include the following points: (1) Americans increasingly place higher requirements on the products that they buy; (2) they embrace novel technological developments with such enthusiasm that business is precipitated into product changes at a rate that jeopardizes production mastery of such changes; and (3) consumers buy and own much more than before. As a result, it is argued, users may have negative quality judgments despite great forward strides in U.S. production quality control.[3]

Which argument is correct, or more correct, need be of no concern at this point. What is of concern is simply that if Americans feel that their goods are not of adequate quality, marketers must strive to correct this impression in order to stay or grow in the American market. And they must cope with some of the government reactions to the quality issue, as manifested in new regulatory and legislative enactments. On this issue, further discussion is reserved for the section on consumerism.

THE QUALITY OPPORTUNITY FOR IMPORTED GOODS

Traditionally, the American consumer has rated the products offered to him on a prestige scale that had imports at both the top and bottom. Certain high-prestige items such as German cameras, French wines, English china, and Scandinavian furniture have been at the top of the quality scale.* Relatively low-priced items from abroad

---

*Importer BK links the precedence of European imports to the general cultural heritage of American purchasers.

have tended to be at the bottom of the scale, with domestic products in between. In general, European countries had the prestige positions; Japan, the only major non-European supplier of manufactured imports before World War II, used to be the major source of low-prestige products.

Japan has accomplished a remarkable change of image in the American market since World War II. Concerted efforts on the part of both public and private groups in that country were successful in supplanting the country's image as a supplier of "cheap" goods.[4] Today, Japanese goods tend at least to be viewed by the American consumer with an open mind. He pays more in many cases for Japanese television sets and cameras than for American-made products and is an enthusiastic purchaser of certain types of durables such as Japanese binoculars, which are highly dependent on a quality reputation for consumer acceptance.[5] Traditional scales have in some cases been reversed, with some Japanese cameras selling at higher prices than their German counterparts.

This precedent may be of some assurance to foreign producers interested in penetrating the U.S. market. The old stereotypes have been overturned. This applies to domestic goods as well as imports; the American motorist's disillusionment with his major-brand automobile means that large expenditures for advertising no longer can safely guarantee a seller against negative quality reactions on the part of the prospect. The opportunity—and the incentive—for quality attainment and preservation for manufactured imports from the developing country should be evident.

QUALITY AS A MATTER OF ABILITY

It is customary to think of the limits of manufacturing ability of developing countries as being determined by matters of capital intensity and advanced technology. Examples of production beyond the reach of most such countries might be petrochemicals and automobiles.* But some of the exportable production abilities of these countries may be set by more subtle factors. Anyone can sit at a piano and pick out a succession of notes, but a symphony or a song requires a composer. To illustrate this analogy in terms of the question at hand,

---

*In the words of importer AA, "the main problem is . . . an inability to make the item at all."

most countries, unless custom forbids, produce some type of alcoholic beverage. But the ability to produce an exportable beer or liquor requires unique skills, painstaking production controls, plus equipment of at least sufficient sophistication to guarantee product and package uniformity.* Capital and technology are involved, but in a much more intricate relationship than might have been supposed.

This technical threshold of exportability must constantly be kept in view, particularly for the American market. Does an aluminum pot or pan that serves the home market of a Latin American country quite adequately have the quality needed to sell in the United States market? Before this can be answered, the product must be carefully compared with what is available on the shelves of U.S. retail stores. If the exporter cannot do this himself, he must rely on the comparison made by the U.S. importer.**

Unfortunately, it is likely that this threshold ability can be negatively affected by import-substitution policies in the developing country. Such policies, which reserve the domestic market in the developing country to domestic producers by insulating them from foreign competition through tariffs or other import restrictions, can establish a production situation in which quality sinks below internationally competitive levels. The question has been raised (importer AP) as to whether an enterprise can successfully produce a product of export quality alongside a product of much lower domestically acceptable quality. The quality threshold of a product is no stronger than its weakest link.

---

*Importer AN reports on the inability of producers in Korea or Taiwan satisfactorily to imitate French handmade barrettes and combs. Importer BW supplied tubular rug machinery to a potential supplier in Korea, but could not secure an adequate product. In some cases, there is some trade-off between price and quality. Importer CB reports that an advantageous price of a Far East product at 80 percent quality acceptability was a better buy than a German product at 85 to 90 percent acceptability; importer CR reports that plywood from Taiwan was inferior to its competition, but sufficiently less expensive.

**Importer CJ has found instances where producers with an adequate home-market product could not furnish output suitable for the U.S. market.

Case History BW-1

A floor covering consisting of fur squares sewn together
that was developed in a South American country (importer
BW). The retail price of the product in the United States
was in the neighborhood of $200 and well worth it, with con-
trasting squares of exquisite textures and colors. Within a
year after sale, however, about 60 percent of the products
were returned to the dealers because the thread used to sew
the squares together was not strong enough, and the rug
broke up into small pieces of fur (the rug producer had been
compelled to use domestically produced thread). Fortunately, the importer was able to convince the government of the
exporting country to permit the importation of strong thread
in place of the domestically produced thread, and subsequent rugs were free of this defect.

There may be many instances in which the incorporation of a
part not made in the exporting country—from the United States or
elsewhere—may be a worthwhile method of production. A pepper mill,
for example, made of beautiful native wood may nevertheless be a
failure in the American market if the grinding mechanism is not well
enough made to withstand reasonable use. If the assembly labor is a
significant cost factor, producing such a product with a mechanism
imported into the producing country may be a way of achieving adequate
quality without sacrificing the necessary competitiveness of the finished
product.[6]

Sometimes the technical problem involved in producing a manufactured product for export from a developing country may be simple
in nature, but solving it may require an extreme measure.

Case History AY-1

The American importer (AY) supplied shoe machinery to
his new Near Eastern supplier and helped to install it. Yet
the first shipment he received was defective—all the shoes
were mounted lopsided on the last. All that was required
was a simple adjustment in the machinery, but when cables
proved ineffective, the importer found it necessary to make
a 6,000-mile trip back to the supplier to do it himself.

QUALITY AS A MATTER OF POLICY

Since the quality of a product is defined as its "degree of excellence," it might appear that quality is synonomous with excellence. Critically interpreted, however, the definition may be said to encompass products whose degree of excellence is low as well as high. The point of this comment is that the foregoing discussion should not be interpreted as a proposal that only those manufactured products of an exceedingly high—read expensive—quality are acceptable to the American market. Many imported products long have, and still do, fill the American market's need for low-priced lines. A child's baseball mitt, a novice's golf clubs, or a housewife's screwdriver are typical consumer products in which the purchaser's desired investment is likely to be as limited as possible. Frequently, domestic products comprise the top of an American distributor's line, and his lower-priced items are from abroad.[7]

Quality is, after all, the equation between the cost of a product and its value in use. A baseball mitt may be expected to wear out in two years, but not to come apart at the seams after the first few uses; the novice's golf clubs may hamper his score after he attains a certain degree of proficiency, but should not break in use; the housewife's screwdriver may have a simple handle, but should be able to cope with the lid of a paint can. The point is that the producer's decision on quality must be taken deliberately, for the purpose of serving well the specific type of market intended. One is reminded of the rueful sign posted by a storekeeper: "This is a nonprofit enterprise; we didn't plan it that way— it just happened."

Bargaining with quality may cost an exporter in a developing country his American trade. If the American importer with whom he is negotiating offers what he considers too low a price for the product, the exporter may be ill advised to take the order and try to make good by cheapening the product. If the resulting inferior product fails to find acceptance from U.S. end-users, both parties lose.*

QUALITY AS A MATTER OF CONSISTENCY

American school children learn about Eli Whitney as the inventor

---

*Importer AZ is concerned about suppliers who seek to secure a share of the market by cutting price at the expense of quality. Importer BN feels that European suppliers will not trade price for quality but that some Asian suppliers will.

of the cotton gin, but his more lasting contribution to world technology may have been his development of interchangeable parts. The muskets Whitney produced in 1798 for the new American government were delivered late, but the principle said to have been employed in building them—that the parts, machine-made to specified tolerances, would fit any one of the guns—became the keystone of modern production. The ability to maintain product consistency is still the sine qua non of efficient manufacturing, and product consistency is what the U.S. end-user expects. Obviously, as previously discussed, this is in part a matter of production ability, and if equipment cannot be adjusted to maintain certain tolerances, many types of products cannot secure market acceptance.*

But certain producers in developing countries seem unimpressed with the need for product consistency. One importer (AK) cautions that suppliers should fill orders in accordance with the sample they submit, not just the way they want to ship it, even if they feel that they have made improvements.** One can visualize the consternation of the purchaser who orders a product based on a sample, only to find the shipment has larger dimensions and cannot fit in the space for which it was intended.

Handicrafts raise some special points with respect to product consistency. Obviously, there is still a large U.S. market for hand-crafted products, although the view has been expressed (importer AJ) that developing countries need to give handicrafts less emphasis in their export goals. The American consumer, who can afford an assortment of mass-produced goods, appears to show an increasing degree of interest in purchasing certain types of handicrafts for their distinctive and aesthetic values. One frequently sees a label bearing such words as "natural variations in this product are to be expected, since it was crafted by hand," but the question remains as to whether these product variations were essential to the handcrafting process or whether they are an excuse for inadequate control of product uniformity.

Failure to smooth the sole edge of a slipper is not a necessary "natural variation" among samples of the product. When product variations are great enough to result in leaky vases or leather products

---

*Importer AB cites an instance where a Mexican supplier could not keep wood containers within the dimensional tolerances required for U.S. users.

**Importer BQ sent quality control people to Taiwan to secure product uniformity.

that come apart in use, the fault is not in the handcrafting, but in the failure to accept the fact that handmade products, like their machine-made counterparts, must be judged in terms of the function they were made to perform. Decorative value should not be used as a shield for shoddy workmanship.*

QUALITY AS A MATTER OF MANAGEMENT

While micrometric measurements, including those performed with isotopes, and elaborate statistical procedures are frequently employed in certain complex manufacturing operations, quality preservation in the production of many simpler lines is still a composite of less-sophisticated matters, including the human relations involved in management. Rightly or wrongly, fairly or unjustly, the most common comment by importers or would-be importers of manufactured goods from the developing nations about quality (a similar complaint is made about packaging) is that "they don't care."**

Case History AB-2

A U.S. importer (AB) had purchased furniture from a south-eastern European exporter, a previously dependable source, for transshipment to a final buyer in the Caribbean. Upon inspection of the cases after they arrived in Houston, it was discovered that all the hardware had been forgotten!

The problem of seeking commitment of new workers to an industrial life has been widely discussed. In some countries, this serves as an encumbrance to the rate of industrialization. "Target workers," for example, who stay in a factory only long enough to earn the where-withal for one or a few prized possessions cannot be motivated in the customary manner of industrial workers.[8] Similarly, the skills of

---

*"Inconsistency" was the problem that prevented importer AQ from purchasing from India, Pakistan, or the Philippines. Importer AC cautions that quality control of handicrafts is limited by the number of trained workers available. Importer BR finds that his supplier of handmade brassware in India has adequate quality control.

**Importer AE mentions that quality involves, among other things, business morality (e.g., shipments must not deliberately be made poorer than samples). Others stressing the managerial option about quality were importers AD, AG, AS, AW, AY, AZ, BL, BN, and BZ.

managers to instruct, to motivate, and to enforce standards of performance that support the achievement of quality are subject to wide variations, particularly in areas where cultural backgrounds may deempha-
size material advancement.

The preceding comments raise questions without answering them.
They are intended, however, to underline the point that production operations in many developing countries may need the infusion of concepts,
ideas, and relationships, rather than sophisticated producing or measur-
ing equipment for the achievement of satisfactory quality.

QUALITY MARKS AND QUALITY STANDARDS

The hallmark of the medieval guild was considered to be the
buyer's guarantee of the quality of a product's manufacture. With the
coming of the mass-production age, the brand of an individual company,
promoted through advertising, served much the same function. The
brand, however, had certain drawbacks. Since it was the possession
of a single firm, the cost of creating and supporting a quality image
in this manner was in many cases excessive for all but the largest
firms. And in international trade, the establishment of a brand image
outside the country of production was a particularly imposing task.

For this reason, groups of firms, or even all the exporting firms
in a single country, have sometimes joined together for the creation
of their own hallmark. The practicality of such an endeavor will depend largely on the ability of the hallmark users to communicate their
efforts at quality control to the purchaser. This might be quite effective in the case of a limited number of industrial purchasers, or it
might be used for a specialized consumer product, such as an optical
item, in which the consumer is expected to be unusually interested in
quality assurance. The very fact, however, that the audience for such
a quality mark is apt to be limited might serve as a warning that promotion of a quality mark without an adequate supporting quality-testing
program may lead to dissipation of the entire investment in this effort.
Users may spread the word among themselves that the mark is not
backed up by the quality it implies.

In the United States, certain quality marks are owned and administered by private organizations. Good Housekeeping, a women's
magazine, awards a "seal of approval" to some of the products advertised in its magazine. Because of increasing public skepticism of the
awarding of such marks to advertisers by a magazine, the publication
added an explicit guarantee that "refund or replacement guaranteed
to consumer if product or performance defective."[9]

The more common type of quality mark or certification is that provided by industrial associations, representing manufacturers, as in the case of the Air Conditioning and Refrigeration Institute, or user interests, as in the case of the American Gas Association. These groups allow their seal to be used if appliances meet their conditions of safety, dependability, performance, etc. The best-known mark of this type is that of the Underwriters Laboratories, as insurance-industry-supported organization whose seal is particularly well known on electrical products, but who also certify the quality of products related to other insurance problems, e.g., resistance to fire, accident, or theft.[10] In some cases, products not carrying the quality mark, whether American made or imported, may be at a competitive disadvantage. It was with this in mind that an official of the U.S. Justice Department's Anti-Trust Division recently indicated that failure to make such a mark available to nonmembers of the sponsoring association could be considered a violation of U.S. anti-trust law.[11]

Related to quality or certification marks in their possible competitive impact, but of a basically different nature, are industrial standards. Because industrial standards are a necessary concomitant of industrial progress, the movement toward standardization in the United States has attained impressive stature.[12] While substantial attention has been given to bringing U.S. national standards into compatibility with standards of other countries, there is still a long way to go in the achievement of internationally recognized standards.[13] An outstanding example of international differences is the fact that metric measurements in the United States are used for only limited purposes, such as in scientific laboratory standards.

The impact of an industrial standard on a manufacturer's output varies. The impact is major if it is a specification standard—e.g., prescribing general homogeneity of products of different manufacturers through a series of design details, maxima and minima of measureable values, etc. There are standards, for example, for softwood plywood. On the other hand, the standard may only rate all products with respect to a given characteristic, such as capacity or power output. Nomenclature standards—prescribing the meaning of given terms—may have little coercive effect toward uniformity, but standards for safety or standards for dimensions (including standards for simplified sizing) may have the effect of keeping a noncomforming manufacturer's output out of an important market.

The possible exclusionary effects of standards relate to the type of product and to the predominant type of buyer. Products that may be characterized as sensitive to regulation, such as foods and drugs, are more apt to bear the brunt of restrictive standards. Similarly, complex products like engines are usually more affected by standards than such casual products as decorative furnishings. At the same time, products sold primarily to industrial, or particularly to federal, state, or local authorities, more typically must conform to applicable American standards.[14] Thus, although voluntary formation of standards through nonprofit organizations is the preferred pattern in the United States, many such standards are less than voluntary when the purchaser insists on them. A further problem is that foreign suppliers are probably not involved in the consultations that take place when standards are developed, and their preferences or suggestions are not involved in the decisions.

In the face of such problems, exporters in developing countries must place heavy reliance on U.S. importers for guidance with respect to American standards. While they may not face some of the problems of suppliers of the most complex types of manufactured imports, such as automobiles, their involvement with standards problems probably will increase in the coming years, as is pointed out in the following section.

THE RISE OF CONSUMERISM

The term "consumerism" has come into vogue in the United States during the past few years to refer to the increasing concern of the American public about everything from the air it breathes to the things it buys. This is not the first time consumer issues have become of wide interest to Americans. During the depression decade of the 1930s, the New Deal administration of Franklin Roosevelt felt it important to name a Consumer Advisory Board to the National Recovery Administration (NRA).[15] There was a renewed interest in consumer cooperatives. And the precursor of today's Consumers Union—an organization established to provide unbiased ratings for its consumer-members—began in that decade (see below).

But until recently, the consumer movement was a minor force in American life. With perhaps the exception of such special areas as credit unions and rural electric cooperatives, the American cooperative movement never attained the importance of the movement in such areas as Scandinavia.[16] And Consumers Union, although it has persisted over the years, in 1967, was still probably regularly read in only one out of every forty families. During the latter half of the 1960s, however, new consumer forces began to be felt. There was Ralph Nader's book Unsafe at Any Speed, which criticized the American automobile, and Rachel Carson's Silent Spring, which warned of the dangers to the natural environment from pesticides.[17] By 1970, a new consumerism had become an established fact for American marketers.

The impact of consumerism is felt directly in the marketplace and indirectly in increased government regulation. In the first instance, publication in the New York Times of a study purporting to show that most American cold cereal breakfast foods are filled with "empty calories" can reasonably be expected to shift sales to the products identified in the study as more nutritious.[18] At the same time, the hearings that sparked this disclosure will add fuel to the fire being built by legislative campaigners for greater controls over consumer products by the federal government. Among the serious aspects of this situation for marketers is the growing use of consumer court suits against product imperfections. Current trends in court decisions may make it easier to press such court actions, and awards for damages could run high.[19]

Some previously unnoticed or little-noticed hazards of consumer products are: compressed-air toys that can deafen a child with their noise, carbon tetrachloride cleaning fluids that can kill users in un-ventilated rooms, glass shower and patio doors that can sever arteries when victims walk into them, electric appliances with excessive shock hazards, toys with edges sharp enough to cut children, and cribs with spaces between slats wide enough to trap a baby's head. One of the greatest concerns has been the flammability of fabrics. It now appears that this concern applies to many standard cotton fabrics as well as to those of special or artificial construction.[20]

The American marketer probably feels himself being squeezed between an increasingly aggressive consumer and, responding to this attitude, an increasingly aggressive attitude by regulatory agencies such as the Federal Trade Commission and Congressional advocates of new legislation. The marketer still has to find the sales impact of consumerism: will consumers pay slightly more for a gasoline from which all or most of the air-polluting lead has been removed? Will consumers buy less attractive products if the loss of attractiveness is due to the incorporation of safety features?

Meanwhile, government regulatory agencies know they have strong public backing for actions taken in the name of the consumer. The best recent example was the prohibition by the Food and Drug Administration of cyclamates in food and drinks, an action that caused enormous inventory losses to American suppliers of such products. But even so mundane a product as an extension ladder comes under government purview—a Federal Trade Commission Trade Regulation Rule requires that advertisements state the safe working length of such ladders, rather than the sum of the lengths of their component parts.[21] Sometimes such rulings may be advantageous to the exporter in the developing country, as when the Commission rules that furniture can't be called "Danish" unless it is made in Denmark or limits the use of the word "mahogany" to certain species of woods.[22] But whatever the impact, government regulation will become a fact increasingly to be faced by all those selling products in the American market.

Consumerism is potentially a deterrent to imports from the developing countries. But it is certainly a golden opportunity for exporters to increase their American sales by concentrating on products that are safer, more natural, less environment-polluting, or less subject to abuse.

SUMMARY

In this chapter, it has been pointed out that the quality of products has become a matter of great current concern in the American market. This may become an opportunity for exporters in developing countries, since the success of the Japanese in raising their quality image means that imported products need not retain any stereotype of second best.

The facets of quality production were then examined. Quality, it appears, may be a matter of ability. But ability is not simply a question of intensity of investment, or sophisticated know-how; it may be a composite of special skill and attention to detail. Above all, producers must understand the quality required by their market and must not use the excuse of handicraft to be inconsistent in the quality or specifications of their products. In sum, concerned people, rather than sophisticated tools or equipment, are typically the critical factor in quality control.

Quality marks of one type or another are used both in the American market and by foreign suppliers to convince buyers of the excellence of different makes of the same type of product or even of all products of one country. Industrial standards are another quality reference point. In both cases, the ability of an exporter to secure the seal or meet the quality may be of key competitive important.

Consumerism, although really not new in the American market, has recently attained a degree of importance that makes it a key factor in many marketing decisions. Imports from the developing countries can be hurt by this situation, or exporters can seek to turn it instead to their own advantage.

NOTES

1. For a presentation on the economic theory of quality, see Lawrence Abbott, Quality and Competition (New York: Columbia University Press, 1955).

2. See "Blue-Collar Blues on the Assembly Line," Fortune, July, 1970, pp. 69-117.

3. This general point of view is expressed in "They Don't Make Cars like They Used to," Quality Assurance, March, 1969, pp. 22-24.

4. For a discussion of the growth of Japanese exports since World War II, see Warren Hunsberger, Japan and the United States in World Trade (New York: Harper & Row, 1964). Specific references to export quality appear on pp. 82, 158, 161-63, and 251. Mr. Hunsberger mentions the influence of U.S. buyers in upgrading the quality of Japanese exports.

5. See Schedule 7, in U.S., Tariff Commission, Summaries of Trade and Tariff Information, TC Publication 322, Vol. II (Washington, D.C., 1970), pp. 35-36. For a discussion of Korean efforts at export quality improvement, see Amicus Most, Expanding Exports: A Case Study of the Korean Experience (Washington, D.C.: U.S. Agency for International Development, 1969), pp. 84-91.

6. An advertisement for a Japanese automobile (New York Times, July 5, 1970, p. 22 S, col. 1) says "One thing you'll love about Datsun is its automatic transmission from Muncie, Indiana."

7. For a discussion of this relationship with respect to baseball gloves, see Schedule 7, in Summaries of Trade and Tariff Information, Vol. IV, pp. 100-103.

8. Country labor studies of some of the primary-commodity-exporting countries appear in Walter Galenson, ed., Labor and Economic Development (New York: Wiley, 1959); and Walter Galenson, Labor in Developing Economies (Berkeley: University of California Press, 1962).

9. For an account of the Good Housekeeping "Institute" and its testing activities in support of the seal of approval, see the New York Times, August 28, 1966, Section III, p. 16, col. 5.

10. U.S., Department of Commerce, National Bureau of Standards, Directory of U.S. Standardization Activities (Washington, D.C.: U.S. Government Printing Office, 1967), pp. 7, 25-28, 46, 229-31.

11. Address of Barry Grossman, Assistant Chief, Evaluation Section, Antitrust Division, Department of Justice, summarized in Journal of Marketing, July, 1970, p. 71.

12. A summary of sources of information on U.S. standardization is E. J. Struglia, Standards and Specifications: Information Sources, Management Information Guide 6 (Detroit: Gale Research Co., 1965).

13. The increasing acceptance of international standards by the United States has been recognized as an urgent requirement for U.S. export expansion. International Commerce, March 9, 1970, p. 5.

14. "At every level of government, standardization insinuates itself in the form of building codes, purchase specifications, grading rules, and many more." Benjamin Melnitsky, Profiting from Industrial Standardization (New York: Conovor-Mast Publications, 1953), p. 12.

15. David Hamilton, The Consumer in Our Economy (Boston: Houghton Mifflin, 1962), p. 313.

16. Cooperative retail establishments accounted for only 1 percent of total U.S. retail sales in 1954. U.S., Department of Labor, Bureau of Labor Statistics, Consumer Cooperatives, Bulletin 1211 (Washington, D.C.: U.S. Government Printing Office, 1957), p. 13.

17. Ralph Nader, Unsafe at Any Speed (New York: Grossman, 1965); Rachel Carson, Silent Spring (Boston: Houghton Mifflin, 1962).

18. New York Times, July 24, 1970, p. 1, col. 6, and p. 38, col. 2.

19. Business Week, July 4, 1970, p. 44.

20. (Senator) W. G. Magnuson and Jean Carper, The Dark Side of the Marketplace (Englewood Cliffs, N.J.: Prentice-Hall, 1968), pp. 128-45.

The National Commission on Product Safety found "unacceptable risks to consumers" among the following products, in addition to those mentioned: color television sets, fireworks, floor furnaces, glass bottles, bicycles, vaporizers, power tools, protective headgear, rotary lawnmowers, unvented gas heaters, and wringer washing machines. Business Week, July 4, 1970, p. 37.

21. Journal of Marketing, July, 1969, p. 69.

22. See the U.S., Federal Trade Commission, Trade Practice Rules for Household Furniture (Washington, D.C., December 18, 1963).

6

**PACKING
AND PACKAGING
MANUFACTURED EXPORTS
FOR THE
AMERICAN MARKET**

THE DISTINCTION BETWEEN PACKING
AND PACKAGING

The packing and packaging of manufactured exports for the American market involves some unique operational challenges and some challenges that are simply typical of international trade. Broadly defined, packing and packaging both involve the physical protection of a product between producer and final consumer. When a distinction is made between the terms, packing is generally considered to be outside wrapping that protects the product from its environment during storage and transportation and packaging is the smallest or most immediate container for the product itself. Many writers do not consider the distinction to be important, because packing and packaging share many characteristics and because the exact borderline between the two is not always easy to define.[1]

In considering manufactured imports from the developing countries, however, the distinction assumes special significance, because packing is the requirement for moving the product through international trade, from developing country to the United States, whereas packaging in the American market has an important promotional function to perform.

Because of this difference in roles between packing and packaging, they are treated separately in the following discussion. Problems between them may be parallel—for example, materials availability, technology, and skills—but the problems are largely on different planes, and the solutions are likely to be achieved in different ways.

INNOVATIVE PACKING FOR
MANUFACTURED EXPORTS

The developing countries are familiar with the requirements of international trade, including those related to packing, for the primary commodities that they regularly export. Such packing requirements in some cases are nonexistent, e.g., for metal or mineral products shipped in bulk or carried in special purpose vessels (petroleum). Or they may be strongly traditional, as in the case of the trade in green coffee or raw cotton.[2] Even in the instance of tea, where elaborate wood chests are used, shippers do not necessarily have the innovative skills to cope with the individualized packing requirements of various manufactured products.

Innovations do occur in the shipping of primary commodities— for example, in the recent introduction of containers for the handling of fresh bananas.[3] Each such innovation, however, probably involves cooperative efforts on the part of producers and shippers on a scale that may be difficult to match in the development of new types of trade in manufactured products.*

In addition to representing a technical problem, sometimes of absorbing complexity, packing for international shipment involves a multivariate cost equation. The economics of packing can defeat incipient trade just as any other uncontrolled production-cost variable can. Overpacking, which may practically eliminate losses due to damage, may place the cost of the delivered product in the American market out of reach of potential buyers. Some costs rise directly in proportion to one another. Certain kinds of more elaborate packing increase both weight and cubage of the shipment; in other cases, one can be traded off against another, with weight probably the most important cost factor for land shipment, cubage for ocean freight.

Air freight is an extreme example of changes in the packing cost equation. The difference between air and ocean shipment from almost all developing countries to the American market must be justified through a series of economies, such as inventory savings, extreme high value with respect to weight, style responsiveness, etc. But when air freight becomes potentially economically possible, the shipper must convert his packing procedures so as to take advantage

---

*In the opinion of importer AJ, packing facilities must be developed at the same time a new product source is developed.

of the lessened handling exposure of air shipment and the astronomic increase in the cost per ounce of packing weight.[4]

U.S. tariffs provide a modest subsidy in the matter of packing expense. Unlike those of practically every other major world market, ad valorem rates—the prevailing type in the U.S. tariff—are, in general, calculated on f.o.b. (country of origin) value, rather than on c.i.f. (country of destination) value, the latter including freight costs.[5] Thus, a 20 percent ad valorem tariff applies to the cost of international freight as well as the cost of the product when shipping to the EEC, but only to the cost of the product when shipping to the United States.

MATERIALS AND KNOW-HOW
PROBLEMS IN PACKING

Materials problems may play an important role in the conversion of export packing from primary products to manufactured goods in the developing country. Major materials, such as lumber, are the first to come to mind, but sometimes minor products, such as cement-coated nails, can be just as critical to the adequate accomplishment of an export packing requirement.[6]

Table 14 shows the distribution of wood resources (or at least developed wood resources) to the extent that these are reflected in U.S. imports from the SDCs. It appears that such resources are distributed quite unevenly. From 16 of the 54 SDCs, there were no imports of wood products in 1968; from an additional 12, imports aggregated less than $50,000. Although 12 supplied wood imports ranging from $1.1 million to $8.7 million each, in only 2 of these cases were wood imports equal to more than 2 percent of total imports from a given SDC.*

Fiberboard is sometimes used in partial and total replacement for wood in exterior shipping containers.[7] There is a U.S. government-prescribed fiberboard heavy-duty packing configuration suitable for many products in ocean shipping.[8] The specifications for adequate fiberboard packing, however, are quite exacting, requiring well-made

----

*Importer AW reports an instance where a Mexican supplier successfully utilized small tree branches as a substitute for wood slats in crating his shipments.

TABLE 14

Imports of Wood Products from SDCs Compared with Total
U.S. Imports from SDCs, 1968
(million dollars)

Country of Origin	Wood Imports	Total U.S. Imports	Wood as Percent of Total U.S. Imports
Afghanistan	--	10.6	--
Lebanon	--	11.3	--
Central African Republic	--	13.0	--
Burundi and Rwanda	--	19.8	--
Uruguay	--	22.0	--
United Arab Republic	--	32.8	--
Malagasy Republic	--	37.4	--
Kuwait	--	39.4	--
El Salvador	--	44.5	--
Ethiopia	--	46.4	--
Uganda	--	51.7	--
Saudia Arabia	--	58.3	--
Pakistan	--	63.9	--
Iran	--	83.4	--
Libya	--	89.7	--
Israel	--	116.8	--
Morocco	a	10.6	b
Paraguay	a	12.3	b
Kenya	a	19.7	b
Tanzania	a	24.6	b
Haiti	a	26.4	b
Liberia	a	51.1	b
Jamaica	a	137.7	b
Dominican Republic	a	156.2	b
Indonesia	a	174.5	b
Republic of Korea	a	198.6	b
Trinidad and Tobago	a	215.4	b
Venezuela	a	949.6	b
Gabon	0.1	13.9	1
Federal Republic Cameroon	0.1	23.7	b
Congo (Kinshasa)	0.1	41.9	b
Panama	0.1	78.5	b
Costa Rica	0.1	88.3	b
Argentina	0.1	206.7	b
India	0.1	312.2	b
Peru	0.2	328.3	b
Bolivia	0.3	30.0	1
Guatemala	0.3	71.0	b
Ceylon	0.4	30.6	1
Chile	0.4	203.1	b
Guyana	0.5	34.0	1
Nigeria	0.5	36.3	1
Mexico	1.1	893.4	b
Nicaragua	1.2	49.7	2
Ivory Coast	1.2	79.1	2
Thailand	1.3	81.0	2
Ghana	1.6	77.7	2
Taiwan	2.1	269.6	1
Ecuador	2.3	89.9	3
Colombia	2.5	264.0	1
Honduras	2.7	82.6	3
Philippines	3.8	435.1	1
Singapore and Malaysia	6.4	268.6	2
Brazil	8.7	669.6	1

[a]Less than $50,000.
[b]Less than .5 percent.

Source: Based on data from U.S. General Imports, Report FT 155, 1968 Annual (Washington, D.C.: U.S. Government Printing Office, 1969).

types of board to provide the necessary combinations of stiffness and cushioning, plus waterproof tape for moisture resistance, and perhaps various additional reinforcing materials. Failure to provide fiberboard packing of such specifications has led to export fiascoes. The demise of certain U.S. exports after World War II has been attributed to the attempt of U.S. producers, confronted with materials shortages, to adapt inadequate fiberboard shipping cartons to an export assignment.[9] Although any packing material, including wood, may require some type of processing or manufacturing undertaking, this production capability becomes much greater when fiberboards are involved. Cost levels of pulp are involved; if no domestic production facilities are available, the board may have to be imported. Many developing countries, however, in their desire to treat the production of fiberboard as a problem of import substitution, may substantially increase its cost or lower its quality, or both, with respect to international levels.* The result is impairment of their potential for exporting new manufactured products.[10]

As previously mentioned, the innovative packing requirements for new manufactured exports from the developing countries may outstrip the know-how available in these countries.** This is not to suggest that such packing methods have attained internationally agreed standards of rationality; despite persistent efforts, such programs as containerization and modular shipping-case sizes have achieved only limited acceptance.[11] But they are illustrative of the types of adaptations that have to be faced in the shipping of internationally-traded manufactured goods.

Because of the substantial labor-input in packing, repacking of products before their delivery to the final point of sale can seriously impair the final price competitiveness. Therefore, there is a substantial advantage to packing methods that can carry products through

-----

*India and Pakistan have been particularly criticized for shortages of cartons (importers AB and BX). Importer AC refers to "fantastic ceramics" which he cannot purchase from South Asia because packing is not available. Carton quality in Taiwan appears to be lower than preferred (importers BL and BQ).

**Importer BH (a mass merchandiser) states that vendors sometimes can meet exacting specifications concerning order quality and timing, yet fail to pack securely.

ocean transportation to the U.S. market and then by land transportation within that market. This imposes on the original shipper additional knowledge burdens, since land-carrier requirements in the U.S. are detailed and explicit.[12] In addition to this, U.S. warehousing has itself undergone a mechanization revolution. Palletization and vertical storage are its chief characteristics. Products that cannot be pallet-loaded for fork-lift truck handling or that cannot be stacked in typical modern warehouse fashion (tiers of up to twenty feet in height) may impose substantial cost penalties on their handlers. (Canned goods are palletized in Thailand for importer CT.)

The availability in the developing country of the materials, as well as the skills, needed for adequate packing is in itself no guarantee that a satisfactory packing job will be done. Exporter management must recognize the critical importance of the packing job and give its performance the attention required. To illustrate in the simplest terms, agreements on explicit types of packing materials and procedures between shipper and recipient are of no avail if the former does not exercise adequate supervision over the carrying-out of the agreed-upon procedures. A package improperly placed within its cushioning material, for example, can easily be damaged during shipment.*

Because the preceding discussion has concentrated on packing problems, the impression may be left that such problems are largely unsolvable. Obviously, this is not the case, since there has been a tremendous increase in manufactured imports from the developing countries. Many importers (BD, BR, BS, and BZ) currently find that packing is "no problem or that damages due to packing failures are down to an "acceptable level" (canned-goods importer CN). In some instances, close supervision and careful instruction by the importer or his representative seem to have brought about this happy state of affairs;** in other cases, a supplying developing country seems to have acquired a substantial group of firms experienced in the diverse requirements of export packing for manufactured goods.***

----

*Importer AY illustrates his belief that suppliers in developing countries frequently consider proper packing "of no importance" by referring to the frequent omission of packing lists with shipments.

**Importers BV and CA (both are divisions of international Japanese enterprises). Also included is importer BN, who refers to the need for "face-to-face" discussion of packing requirements.

***Importers BL and CS refer to Taiwan in this respect, the latter also mentioning Korea.

PACKAGING AND CHANNELS
OF DISTRIBUTION

Like the packing case, a package is the product's enclosure and physical protection. Such an explanation of the package in today's American market, however, completely misses a prime aspect of its marketing significance—the package is a major promotional tool in U.S. selling.[13]

The promotional function of the American package can be understood by considering the product-display function in selling. The sales clerk who removes a pearl necklace from its showplace within a glass jewelry case and places it before the prospects on a black velvet counter mat is promoting the sale of the necklace through display. Through a stretch of the imagination, the mechanization of the clerk's promotional function can be visualized in the form of a transparent package that would display the necklace to the shopper walking through a self-service store. The transfer of the display function from clerk to package can be viewed as the mechanization of part of the sales-promotion function, in the same way that advertising replaces a salesman's visit to a customer.[14] The package is, in this sense, the completion of the advertising function at the point of sale.

While the self-service concept applies fundamentally to retail selling, the self-service and prepackaged style of selling has so dominated the American market place that many types of industrial products have packaging requirements similar to those of consumer goods. Industrial consumables such as drill bits are packaged for shelf selection, as are many types of commercial and office supplies, and self-service shopping is sometimes practiced in outlets handling these types of products.[15]

Not all goods, of course, are packaged. Certain products do not by their nature lend themselves to packaging. Those that are too cumbersome to be displayed via packaging, such as furniture and lamps, must be displayed in traditional ways. At the opposite extreme are items that can be displayed simply and naturally for self-selection without packaging, such as clothing.

Both of these types of examples emphasize that packaging is not a matter of the immediate container—all types of products may need some type of immediate container, for example, to break quantities up into those customarily traded. But the packaging phenomenon in the American market is a display and sales-promotional one, rather than a physical matter of enclosure. Products that are frequently or typically sold packaged in the American market are not, however, invariably handled in this manner. For them, packaging may be viewed rather as a key to wider distribution.

A carton of soap flakes is packaged because of its nature, but a desk ornament need not be.[16] The latter may be sold in any one of the increasing number of specialty retail import houses throughout the United States.[17] The growth of such outlets can be illustrated by inspecting the classified telephone directories of many major American cities. Under the heading "Importers," a number of the listings may be found to be retail stores—sometimes specializing by country (e.g., Mexico) and sometimes by product (e.g., dinnerware—but attracting the major part of their clientele by the frank appeal of the foreign origin of their products.

The author has seen, in outlets of this type, products ranging from fireplace tools to slide rules displayed in open bins. Many of the products carried by such outlets are packaged. The stores, however, are typically set up to handle and display unpackaged products as well. The unpackaged format lends itself particularly well to the bargain hunter, but an inspection of products in bins may reveal that a substantial proportion have been noticeably damaged, perhaps before being displayed or in the process of being handled by shoppers.

In contrast to specialty outlets, a visitor from another country might be hard put to distinguish (from the inside) between an American grocery supermarket (especially with nonfood departments), a department store, a variety store, a discount department store, a mail-order-company-run department store, or a large drug store. All such outlets operate on the self-service system in most departments, and the packaged product is their standard item; sales help, if available at all, is usually scarce, and the main function of store personnel is to secure payment for the purchase. This type of selling now accounts for the vast majority of American retail purchasing.*

In sum, the packaged product furnishes entree to the major portion of American retail selling space. Packaging is often considered just as essential for products sold under special circumstances, including many business-type items.

—————————————

*Importer BM says that packaging is enormously important in the areas of "imitative goods" (presumably distinguishing them from handicrafts, which are favorite products for import-specialty stores).

PACKAGING PROBLEMS

The problems of the developing countries with respect to packaging are of nature similar to those described with respect to packing, but of a generally greater magnitude.*

Case History BW-2

The product, a novelty stair-tread (floorcovering) made in Southeast Asia, was adequately packaged, but in a carton much larger than necessary, because the proper size was not available in the country of origin. The importer (BW) had to drop the item because retail stores refused to handle the cumbersome package.

Natural materials like wood are rarely used for packaging. Instead, there is a great demand for such products as specialty papers and sophisticated plastics, rarely obtainable from local production in the developing countries.[18] Production techniques are more involved. American packages in current use frequently depend for eye appeal on complex techniques such as over-printing on plastic films.[19] Even the typical label for canned food requires a high degree of perfection in color-printing techniques.**

Finally, package design is a highly technological function in American marketing, and the skills of the best designers are in demand much in the same way as the skills, say, of electronic data-processing consultants. The developing countries will have to import a good portion of such skills in the near future, because of the time needed to train local personnel up to such skills and, in some cases, because the need for such skills may be limited to part of the export sector. Especially in the case of products for which packaging

---

*The problem, in the view of importer BA, is that U.S. packaging has made such strides in the past decade that overseas suppliers have difficulty in comprehending our requirements. A "beautiful" foreign product may be unsaleable because of poor packaging.

**Importer CN refers to the great progress made in label printing in Taiwan; importer CT states that good labels can now be printed in Thailand.

is highly competitive in the American market, package design can best be imported by securing it from the American buyer. If design requirements are not as exacting, local preparation may be possible.

As in other fields, mechanization is proceeding rapidly in American packaging practice. Packaging in the developing countries is still largely characterized by hand operations. In its April, 1969, review of world packaging trends, Modern Packaging magazine referred to Singapore's hand-sealing and hand-labeling of cosmetic products as typical of Asian packaging.

Much as theoretical economic considerations might dictate the desirability of high-labor-factor operations in developing countries, technology is still quite uneven in certain types of packaging, and hand operations cannot efficiently be substituted for packaging machinery if certain types of products are to be economically produced. Food products are frequently an example of this fact.* In such cases, governments of developing countries may need to recognize that their ability to export may be dependent on their ability to secure packaging as well as production machinery for products they hope to export.

One alternative to packaging manufactured products that are exported from developing countries is to repackage such products on their arrival in the United States. There are some types of food products that have traditionally been imported in bulk and placed in immediate containers upon arrival in the United States.[20] In at least one case, the U.S. tariff appears to penalize prepackaging.** Greater flexibility can be obtained in processing steps concerning imports when such steps are performed within a free port or foreign trade zone. Substandard merchandise does not have to be passed through customs, and payment of duties can be deferred until the packaged product is ready to enter the U.S. market.

Comparative advantage in the trading of manufactured goods,

----

*Food packaging can raise difficult production problems. Importer CT imports frozen seafood in bulk packages because the hygienic problems of inaugurating retail packaging in Asia are still considered too great in view of U.S. Food and Drug Administration standards.

**The most-favored-nation rate for blue-mold cheese is higher by 5 percent ad valorem if not imported "in original loaves."

however, can be obtained most readily through lower labor costs. If a substantial portion of a product's labor costs must be paid for at U.S. rates, the advantage can disappear. Table 15 presents estimates of what packaging of American products costs as a percent of total product cost. These figures are open to substantial question because of the degree to which they represent speculative estimates.[21] Nonetheless, it must be clear that, for many types of manufactured products, packaging represents so significant a part of total cost that its transfer to the United States may be economically impractical.*

HOW THE PACKAGE SELLS

In a simplified sense, a package "sells itself" in two different types of ways: by selling the contents to the prospect directly, or by selling the prospect on the reputation of the brand name affixed to the package. To create an imaginary example, two cans of asparagus may stand side by side on the shelf of an American supermarket. One can, which can be called Brand X to indicate that the brand name has no connotation to the prospective purchaser, shows a delightful illustration of long, thin, almost pure white asparagus spears, with a title emphasizing these delectable features. The second can simply says S.S. Pierce Top Quality Asparagus. The second can emphasizes the brand name (a long-established American food trademark held in considerable esteem), partly by the entire color scheme and design of the can label. Both packages may sell very well, the first because the label is a direct expression of the promise of the product,[22] the second because the trade name implies quality through the maker's reputation for delivering it.

Imported products have long represented some of the most distinguished brands in the American market—e.g., Rolls Royce automobiles. Before World War II, it may have been assumed that only Western Europe could supply such a successful brands; since then, such products as Sony radios and Nikon cameras have shown that buyer confidence could be built for products from another part of the globe. But the construction of a successful brand name in the American market is doubtlessly a long and very expensive undertaking, one rarely to be attempted for imports from the developing countries in the near future. It is likely, therefore, that "selling the

_____

*In the words of importer AZ, domestic repackaging "sometimes puts the item out of line price-wise."

TABLE 15

Cost of Packaging, Selected Products

Product	Packaging Cost as Percent of Manufacturer's Selling Price
Inks and adhesives	40.0
Cosmetics and toiletries	36.3
Drugs	35.2
Motor oil	34.0
Beer	30.0
Foods	24.1
Candy	21.2
Stationery	20.0
Wax polishes	15.0
Paints	12.5
Toys	9.1
Cigars	8.0
Baked goods	7.8
Meats	6.5
Liquor	5.2
Automotive parts	5.0
Cutlery	5.0
Hardware	4.0
Office machines	1.4

Source: L. M. Guss, Packaging Is Marketing (New York: American Management Association, 1967), p. 50

product" is apt to be the technique used for packaging by exporters in the developing countries. Fortunately, there appears to be increasing acceptance of this approach in the American market.

One particularly common area where product promotion rather than brand promotion has been the rule is in the case of "private brands."[23] Such brands are the property of large distributors,

ranging from Sears Roebuck, the mail-order firm, to A & P, the
grocery chain. Many of these firms display their private brands side
by side with nationally advertised brands. Their brands sell because
they are promoted by direct advertising (that is, retail ads that include
prices) as distinguished from generalized quality advertising, which
is still largely used for nationally advertised brands. They are also
promoted by display and price promotion within the store.

It may be argued that private brands are indistinguishable in
their appeal from nationally advertised brands because the buyer
feels the maker (or distributor) stands behind both. But the private
brand is under the control of the store in which it sells, and the
exporter in the developing country is perhaps more likely to have the
opportunity of supplying a private-brand commodity. There is, of
course, nothing to prevent the supplier of a nationally advertised
product from buying abroad; but he probably has substantial investments in U.S. production facilities and may fear the effect on buyers
of the required import label "Made in . . . ."

CURRENT PACKAGING TRENDS

Current trends in packaging in the U.S. market are somewhat
contradictory. Producers continue their customary search for cost-
reduction techniques. Canned products, for example, are packed in
containers using tin-free steel or even in substitute cans made more
cheaply from such materials as aluminum foil and fiberboard.[24]
At the same time, the consumer's search for built-in services in the
affluent but labor-short U.S. economy finds its reflection in more
elaborate packaging. Canned liquids now have "pop top" openers
that do not need can openers. Salt cartons are now almost invariably
equipped with dispensing spouts. Reusable packages range from
polyethylene canisters for ice cream to rigid plastic boxes for
stationery, and although many cost considerably more, consumers
frequently are willing to pay the premium, especially when the
highest-quality product is packed in the reusable container. In some
cases, reusability can be added to a simple package, such as by
equipping a blow-molded plastic bottle with a metal rather than an
easily breakable plastic cap. An example of the elaborateness of
some of the built-in services currently being offered in the American
market is a brand of shoe polish (Kiwi) that is sold as an ensemble
complete with applicator and polishing cloth within a rigid plastic
resealable cup.

Exporters in the developing countries presumably will rarely if ever be in a position to invest resources in pioneering packaging applications. Accordingly, extreme trends in the American market will have to be disregarded in favor of "middle majority" approaches. The danger to imports is that some package convenience, such as a pouring spout, will have become the sine qua non of the American market, and the imported product will be unsalable because of its lack of this feature.[25]

Choice of the size of a package when sizing is not in natural units, as with a pair of shoes, may require careful consideration when penetrating the American market. Convenience has dictated increasing use of portion sizes in such items as food products, i.e., amounts small enough for an individual serving. Domestic packaging in developing countries frequently already takes this form (two aspirin tablets in a package, for example) as a way of catering to the needs of the low-income market. This is where the distinction occurs with the affluent American market. Miniaturization takes place for convenience rather than cost. Thus, the small (six fluid ounce) can of tomato juice will most likely be sold banded together in a "six-pack." Similar paperboard or plastic overlays sell "multi-pack" packages of everything from beer to anti-freeze coolant for automobiles. But super-sized packages have also made a strong appearance. Detergents may be sold in five-pound "tubs." Enormous toy packages are not uncommon. The exporter or would-be exporter should pay special attention to package-size choice since his may be an area selected for attack on "size proliferation" (see below).

LEGAL REQUIREMENTS FOR
PACKAGING AND LABELING

The legal standards for packaging in the American market can appear very formidable for the new exporter. Some of the legislation is common to other countries, whether developed or developing. But there is no substitute for familiarity with specific standards.* For example, laws against deceptive packaging are common to many countries. But what some markets may accept as normal trade styling of packages—for example, a sham bottom for a wine bottle—may be ruled as deceptive and therefore unacceptable under current U.S. federal law. Deliberate slack-filling of packages is obviously deceptive,

----

*Alcoholic beverages probably represent one of the most demanding types of manufactured products for the exporter in the developing country. Importer AW refers to improper labeling, use of "illegal" bottles, and improper fill as common problems.

but it may require unusual care to attain the completeness of package
fill now legally required under American law. A carton for a tube of
toothpaste may be considered deceptively large because the tube is
not inserted diagonally within the carton.

The newest evidence of what is referred to in the United States
as consumerism are the provisions of the 1966 Fair Packaging and
Labeling Act (FPLA) against "undue proliferation" of package sizes.
Consumer groups argued that supermarket shelves were filled with
odd-sized packages in such amounts as 10 3/4 ounces, 2 pounds 3 1/2
ounces, etc., so as to make price comparisons impossible. Many
sizes were deliberately chosen, it was felt, to conceal price increases.
Under the provisions of the FPLA, the Department of Commerce is
authorized to develop, for any industry in which proliferation may be
considered to exist, a voluntary limitation on package sizes. Table
16 gives a list of products for which such standards have been agreed
to.

There are no mandatory provisions at the time of writing against
package-size proliferation. The Department of Commerce may ask
for such power where it feels that voluntary controls are not adequate.
The Department, however, reported that producers contacted "without
exception" had agreed voluntarily to work on package-size limitations.[26]
Nonetheless, the marketer in the developing country should be aware
of voluntary programs, to guard if possible against the use of a nonstandard package. Even where compliance with the standards remains
voluntary, some distributors in the United States may be concerned
about buyer resistance to nonstandard sizes. Sizing problems may
be particularly uncomfortable for some suppliers in developing countries to cope with, because the United States is rapidly becoming
almost the only remaining major world market using English rather
than metric standards of measurement.

Labeling problems are an integral consideration in package
design. Here there can clearly be no substitute for the guidance of
an experienced American importer in such matters as marking the
country of origin, avoidance of conflicts with established U.S. trademarks, the use of idiomatic American English for labeling, and so
forth.* Even experienced hands occasionally make labeling errors.

————————————

*Importer BW refers to an instance when expensive relabeling
was required for floor coverings because the exporter used "illegal"
paper labels in disregard of instructions. Labeling requirements
for marks of origin are established under Section 1304, Title 19, of
the U.S. Code (Customs Regulations 11.8-11.13).

TABLE 16

Standard Package-Size Agreements Secured by the Department of Commerce, January, 1970

Product	Previous Number of Package Sizes	Agreed Number of Package Sizes
Adhesive bandages	37	10
Dry breakfast cereals[a]	33	16
Cheese	22	14
Cookies and crackers	73	56
Dry detergents[b]	22	3
Facial tissues, 1 and 2 ply	16	13
Gift wrapping	n.a.	n.a.
Instant coffee	10	8
Instant tea	12	4
Jellies and preserves	16	10
Macaroni products	32	16
Mayonnaise and salad dressing	12	9
Paper napkins	18	13
Paper towels	33	8
Peanut butter	30	12
Pickles	35 percent reduction	
Potato chips	33 percent reduction	
Refrigerated dough products	24 percent reduction	
Salad and cooking oils[c]	15	7
Soft drinks	33 percent reduction	
Syrups	20 percent reduction	
Tea bags	11	7
Toilet tissues	16	11

[a]Excluding individual serving boxes.
[b]Heavy-duty and normal density.
[c]Excluding olive oils.

Source: Office of Weights and Measures, National Bureau of Standards.

Case History AB-1

An advertising agency wanted a giveaway item,
a paper hat to be distributed at bars as a novelty, to bear
the name of the client—"Old American Whiskey" (a fictitious
name for purposes of this discussion). The agency supplied
a model, which the importer (AB) forwarded to his Japanese
supplier. Samples were returned by the supplier, an experienced firm in this type of work, and accepted by the
importer after having been approved by the advertising
agency and its client. Only after production quantities
arrived did the importer actually open up one of the folded
hats and put it on his head. The legend read "Old American
Whiskey" and then, just below, the required notice "Made
in Japan."

The FPLA codifies certain requirements relating to weight and
ingredient labeling, specifying the placement of such information, the
size of type that must be used, and similar requirements. Federal
Trade Commission regulations (Section 500.5) under the FPLA require that the name and address of the producer or distributor appear
on the label of a consumer commodity. Exporters should keep in mind
that the importer wants his identification on the package rather than
theirs, to forestall efforts by American merchants to buy direct from
an importer's overseas source (importer BL).

Many exporters or would-be exporters who find the new FPLA
provisions formidable to deal with may be somewhat reassured by
the fact that the federal government has an announced policy of
superseding, to the extent practical, separate (and, therefore, frequently conflicting) laws on such subjects by the fifty American states.
Considerable progress in this direction reportedly has been achieved.[27]

SUMMARY

In this chapter, a distinction was drawn between packing and
packaging problems for manufactured imports from the developing
countries. The problems of these countries were described as the
difficulty of coping with innovative packing requirements for manufactured exports, materials availability, and the need for recognition
by exporter management of the importance of adequate packing.

The promotional importance of the package in the American
market was discussed. While packaging problems were found in

certain respects to be similar to packing problems, the sophistication of the materials and techniques were typically considered to be much greater for packaging. Unpackaged products may be limited to specialized channels of distribution in the American market, and repackaging in the United States may make the final product too expensive for competition.

Selling the product rather than selling the brand was suggested to be the more practical approach for packaging most manufactured imports from the developing countries. Private brands typically involve this approach. Current American packages strive for the somewhat contrary goals of low cost and high convenience. Mechanization of packaging in the United States is quite advanced.

Finally, exporters of manufactured products in the developing countries need to be aware of the range of legal constraints on packaging and labeling in the United States. The FPLA, for example, permits the establishment of specific standards in labeling and authorizes a voluntary program for the avoidance of package-size proliferation.

NOTES

1. See, for example, E. J. McCarthy, Basic Marketing: A Managerial Approach (3d ed., Homewood, Ill.: R. D. Irwin, Inc., 1968), p. 225.

2. "The packing of many commodities (e.g., coffee bags, tea cases, and cotton bales) exported from developing countries is subject to detailed international agreements, and many shipping lines and insurance companies will refuse these goods if packed otherwise." International Trade Center, The Role of the Freight Forwarder in Developing Countries (Geneva: UNCTAD/GATT, 1969), p. 15.

3. "Winning Back a Vanishing Market," Printers Ink, June 26, 1964, p. 53.

4. For a general discussion of air-freight economics, see H. T. Lewis, J. W. Willton, and J. D. Steele, The Role of Air Freight in Physical Distribution (Boston: Graduate School of Business Administration, Harvard University, 1956), pp. 104-15.

5. U.S., Bureau of Customs, Exporting to the United States (Washington, D.C.: U.S. Government Printing Office, 1969), p. 20.

6. See Marine Service Department, Insurance Company of North America, "Loss Prevention Recommendations for Export Shipments," reproduced in Philip MacDonald, Practical Exporting and Importing (2d ed., New York: Ronald Press, 1959), pp. 143-48.

7. For a discussion of the use of alternative types of exterior shipping containers, see L. J. Switz, "Packing for Export," International Trade Forum (International Trade Center, UNCTAD/GATT, Geneva), December, 1967, pp. 30-32.

8. See U.S., Defense Supply Agency, Preservation, Packaging, and Packing of Military Supplies and Equipment, DSAM 4145.2, Vol. II (Washington, D.C.: October, 1967) p. 115.

9. MacDonald, Practical Exporting, p. 439.

10. Korea and Mexico are among the countries criticized for high protective tariffs on packaging materials that interfere with economical packaging. Modern Packaging, April, 1969, pp. 153, 163.

11. See "Global Standards: Tug of War," Modern Packaging, April, 1969, pp. 182-84.

12. See, for example, the parcel-post requirements in Preservation, Packaging, and Packing of Military Supplies and Equipment, p. 86.

13. The director of package design for Paper Mate pens says, "The primary objectives of a package are to protect, to identify, and, most important, to sell." Package Design and Its Management (New York: American Management Association, 1965), p. 16.

14. Despite the emphasis in the U.S. market on advertising and related forms of promotion, the Folding Paper Box Association in 1956 reported that 96 food and grocery firms spent 10 percent of their sales revenue for packaging and only 6 percent for advertising and other promotion. Marketing Research Report on Packaging (New York: American Management Association, 1957), p. 3.

15. David L. Luke III, President of the West Virginia Pulp and Paper Co., puts it this way: "The concept of packaging which is so deep-seated in consumer markets has begun to reach levels of comparable sophistication in industrial markets, a trend that is almost certain to gain momentum in the years ahead. The drab and unimaginative packaging which once typified industrial products is rapidly giving way to creative packages designed to mirror the image of the manufacturer and to provide the user of the product with many of the convenience features of consumer packaging." Profitability and Penetration Through Packaging (New York: American Management Association, 1965), p. 2.

16. In many cases, packaging has literally created the products According to the U.S. Department of Agriculture, about 40 percent of the domestic potato crop is processed and packaged. There was little, if any, packaging or processing thirty years ago. A packaging specialist found over twenty types of processed packaged potatoes carried by a supermarket firm. Packaging Considerations for the Marketing Man (New York: American Management Association, 1966), p. 19.

17. Details of one of the most successful of such import houses— Cost Plus Imports of San Francisco—appeared in the New York Times, May 16, 1962, p. 36, col. 1.

18. U.S. and Japanese plastics producers have apparently vigorously promoted some of their products, such as films, in some of the developing countries, probably with favorable effect on local packaging methods. Modern Packaging, April, 1969, pp. 159, 162.

19. A discussion of printing processes, including advantages and limitations, currently used for packaging in the United States appears in the Modern Packaging Encyclopedia (New York: McGraw-Hill, July, 1969), pp. 64-66.

20. Before 1966, "virtually all" imported olives entered the United States in bulk containers (over nine pounds). Despite the beginning of prepackaging in Spain in 1966, over 98 percent of Spanish exports to the United States that year remained in bulk pack. U.S., Tariff Commission, Olives: Report on Investigation 332-51 (Washington, D.C., 1967), pp. 2, 53.

21. Discussion with Mr. Richard Blassey, Packaging Branch, U.S. Business and Defense Services Administration, March 10, 1970.

22. Consumers can be "almost appallingly literal" in their expectations of products based on package illustrations: an instance is reported where an illustration change cut sales in half. D. W. Twedt, "How Much Value Can Be Added Through Packaging?," Journal of Marketing, January, 1968, p. 58.

23. "Private Label Objective: Sell the Product Not the Brand," Modern Packaging, September, 1969, pp. 96-97. See also "The Package and the Product," International Trade Forum, December, 1969, p. 14.

24. Modern Packaging Encyclopedia, p. 264.

25. Stressing the importance of keeping up with competition, a leading American packaging specialist says, "The first step in any packaging project should be to go shopping." Jerome N. Mitchell in Profitability and Penetration Through Packaging, p. 16.

26. U.S., Department of Commerce, Report to the Congress by the Secretary of Commerce on Activities Under the Fair Packaging and Labeling Act During Fiscal Year 1968. (Washington, D.C.: Department of Commerce, 1968), p. 5.

27. Ibid., p. 2.

7

DISTRIBUTION: PATHWAY FROM PRODUCER
TO END-USER

In marketing terms, distribution may be defined as the process of getting a product from the producer to the end-user.[1] In international trade, and more particularly in the trade covered by this study, the distribution process is complicated by the distance between producer and end-user, not merely in geographic terms, but in terms of the differing cultures and institutions in the developing country and in the United States. A frequently made observation by importers contacted during the course of this study (importers AE, AS, AY, BA, BN, BW) was that failure by suppliers in developing countries to understand U.S. distribution was a significant obstacle to the expansion of their manufactured exports. One importer (BX) was generally pessimistic on the subject of getting suppliers to understand distribution in the United States: "We have enough difficulty in explaining to Europeans . . . how distribution works in the United States . . . without venturing into [such countries as] India and Pakistan with the same incomprehensible tale."

The key problem in achieving desirable distribution is in matching up the needs and resources of buyer and seller. Perhaps it is easier to describe this by giving examples of what is not adequate distribution:

1. When the distributor wants too large a quantity for his supplier to deliver

2. When the supplier does not have distributors who are able to buy the quantity of output he is in a position to sell them

117

3. When the distributor does not have customers for the type of product that his supplier can furnish

4. When the distributor requires for his customers a type of product that his supplier cannot furnish

5. When the distributor cannot or does not wish to promote the type of product, or to promote it to the extent necessary to sell a desirable quantity, that his supplier can furnish.

In terms of the number of marketing transactions between producer and distributor, some distribution chains are larger than others. A producer in a developing country selling direct to a mass-merchandising importer is only one step removed from the final purchaser; if he sells to an industrial importer, he is selling direct to the end-user. But this does not mean that such a shorter distribution chain is more efficient in serving the producer's purposes.[2] One comment made by several importers (AA, AB, AK, AZ, BD, BL) was that producers in developing countries would be much more likely to succeed in their efforts to export to the United States if they would use an export agent in their own country. Although such an agent in effect adds another link to the distributive chain, he is a specialist in exporting and can cope with many of the technicalities (see Chapter 8), he may be much more competent to deal in English with U.S. customers, and he understands such problems as complaints for damage in shipment that a producer may be unable to handle.

Indeed, in some cases it is likely that the most efficient distributive chain would not only involve an export agent in the developing country, but a primary importing distributor in the United States, who might in turn sell to other distributors in certain areas. These in turn sell to various types of retailers, from which the end-users would buy. To remain in business, however, these additional distributors would have to perform their functions without raising the final price to the buyer to a noncompetitive height.

This chapter initially differentiates between the major types of purchasers in the United States for manufactured imports from developing countries: mass-merchandising firms, specialist importers and industrial importers. Suppliers in developing countries must make a choice among these three types of purchasers. The chapter then proceeds to discuss certain principles of market segmentation, which should be understood by the supplier in the developing country, even though he himself will have little or no direct involvement in them. His need for understanding is a function of his need to choose an importer or importers and of his need to be aware of the marketing problems they in turn will face in selling his products. Finally, the chapter deals with matters either identified by importers as problem areas or of special interest in connection with their purchases, or attempted purchases, of manufactured products from the developing countries exclusivity of distribution, problems of pricing, and the role of sales promotion.

MASS-MERCHANDISING VERSUS
SPECIALIST IMPORTERS

The mass-merchandising importer may be defined as an organization purchasing for eventual sale through one or a number of large retailing organizations, such as department stores, mail-order firms, supermarket chains, or similar establishments.[3] In most cases, the mass-merchandising importer is a buying department of such an integrated operation, with purchase and final sale to the end-user being made by the same company (for example, Sears Roebuck and Co.), but a mass-merchandising importer may have an agent relationship to a group of large retailing organizations, such as department stores, and purchase for their account. In any event, the mass-merchandising importer most likely purchases a wide range of products, whose only link to one another is that they are sold through the same type of large retail outlets.

The specialist importer, by contrast, deals with a relatively limited line of products, such as shoes, floor coverings, canned goods, and china and crystal, and, in some cases, may be experienced in importing from only certain parts of the world. While this definition can encompass retailers who do their own importing, the following discussion will deal only with importers who import for resale to others who sell wholesale or retail (see the discussion of importer-retailers in Chapter 6).

In dealing with specialist importers, larger suppliers in developing countries should assure themselves that the different potential markets for which their products are intended are all covered. According to one such importer (AK):

A single importer normally concentrates on one field.
. . . For instance, we sell decorative accessories and
cater to interior decorators. Many of our foreign factories manufacture gift items, collectors' items, and

housewares in conjunction with their decorative accessories. [Such a manufacturer] should sell to no less
than four importers and if any of the importers has
less than nationwide distribution, he should sell to more.

Many of the specialist-importing firms are dominated by one or a few
personalities whose trading backgrounds may go back a number of
decades. Typically, these personalities have used intensive personal
contact to develop a group of experienced suppliers in one or more
parts of the world; furnishing a particular type of product to the
American market. In many cases, the specialist-importing buyer
spends as much as half of each year traveling to the countries that
supply him. Unlike the buyers for mass-merchandising organizations,
who usually buy from both domestic and foreign sources, the specialist-
importing buyer buys only from abroad.

The mass-merchandising importer is a large-volume buyer,
both in quantity and in the variety of the products he buys; on the
other hand, he is neither a pioneer in introducing new products, as a
general rule, nor does he have the depth of experience of the typical
importing specialist.* When mass-merchandising organizations have
requirements for small-quantity imports or for imports of relatively
(to them) exotic products, they are apt to buy from the specialist
importers, who sell only at wholesale. On the other hand, the bulk-
import needs of the mass-merchandising importer, for clothing,
novelties, durables, etc., that can be advantageously secured abroad
are purchased directly. The size of such imports in certain parts of
the world is so large that mass-merchandising importers frequently
maintain one or more overseas buying offices.

The specialist importer is most likely the one who develops a
new source of merchandise—that is, a supplier of a new type of imported products, a supplier who has not previously sold the United
States, or a supplier in a country that has not previously sold to the
United States the type of product in question.

The mass-merchandising importer begins buying direct when
a particular foreign location has become established for a type of

---

*The discussion that follows is based on the writer's interviews
with representatives of mass-merchandising organizations. The draft
was reviewed by several of those interviewed, but the writer assumes
responsibility for the interpretations presented.

product (e.g., transistor radios from Japan or sport shirts from Hong Kong). He typically calls for a product that is fairly conventional in design in terms of what the country has previously supplied the American market. Although he may furnish his own design, it is probably not very different from what the foreign exporter has sold in the past. The mass-merchandising importer is quite demanding in questions of quality, adequacy of packing and labeling, and so forth. But his most demanding requirements are doubtlessly in two respects: the large quantity of the purchase (other than for possible trial orders, the mass merchandising importer is the big volume buyer in his product line), and the date on which it must be delivered.

While all American importers are closely controlled by the seasonal demand patterns for their merchandise (not only for clothes, but for holiday products, toys, most types of durables, and so on), the mass-merchandising importer has two additional factors to contend with, when contrasted with most specialist importers. First, he services stores that must plan to the day for their advertising and other sales-promotion activities; second, since his organization is responsible for moving the goods all the way from the pier to the retail counter, storage of excess stocks becomes especially burdensome and must be minimized.

It is possible to theorize about the relationship of exporters in developing countries to specialist importers and mass-merchandising importers as follows (always keeping in mind that these are generalizations, and individual instances may be substantially at variance to them). The exporter is likely to begin trading with the specialist importer. Especially if the product is a new one as far as trade between the two countries is concerned, the development of the exporter-importer relationship is apt to take place over a number of years, and sometimes the trade does not succeed on a permanent basis.

Some of the exporters who become strong and large bid for and secure orders from the mass-merchandising importers. The volume is larger per transaction, but the competitive requirements of this type of business exert downward pressure on the unit price. Nonetheless, this is the take-off into the mass market. For some types of products, this stage never comes. For others, it becomes the established channel for most of the imported merchandise. Perhaps the most usual situation is when mass-merchandising and specialist importers operate side by side, with the latter more likely to be catering to submarkets that are characterized by special distribution patterns, that demand unusual price lines, or that in other ways are somewhat set aside from the middle majority portion of the mass market.

Because the mass-merchandising importer is not an import specialist, his buying generally is done by people who are not import specialists. Imports may constitute only 5 percent of the total sales of the mass merchandiser. Regular buyers are sent on foreign itineraries as part of their annual buying programs to make purchases of import merchandise of their types of goods (e.g., the toy buyer shops for toy imports, the infants'-wear buyer shops for infants' wear). It is not unusual for this buying to be compressed into just a two- or three-week trip.

The function of the sometimes well-staffed foreign buying offices of the mass-merchandising importer is to prepare for the annual visits of the buyers and to follow up after them. For example, the Hong Kong office, informed in advance of the types of purchases to be made, lines up proposed sources, after having made certain checks as to their reliability. After the buyer makes the purchase commitments, the Hong Kong office will follow up on fulfillment of the orders.

Because there is a limit to the number of overseas offices that mass-merchandising importers can establish and because many buyers are understandably reluctant to multiply the number of stops they must make, small countries—and this can apply to Switzerland as well as to Thailand—may suffer a disadvantage in getting their products purchased by mass-merchandising importers. At least one major firm has taken pains to make its offices regional centers for purchasing the products of various countries to overcome this problem.

Mass merchandisers are typically devotees of "committee management." Buying decisions generally stem from the agreement of a group of people in the company; therefore, daring departures, unusual originality, or leadership in merchandise or style trends is much less apt to be their forte. Instead, they represent the mass market in America, offering to the public the type of products that people are ready and willing to buy in quantity. For such products, the delivery time must be right, the quality must be adequate, the product must be of a type that will largely sell itself (because skilled retail salesman are usually not involved in the final sale), the volume must be high, and the price must be low enough to move the merchandise rapidly off the shelves. The conditions are demanding, but the rewards, in terms of big orders for the suppliers, are substantial.

INDUSTRIAL IMPORTERS

Manufactured industrial-type imports—such as machinery items, industrial parts, components, subassemblies, etc.—may be imported by specialist importers and resold through them to U.S. manufacturers or to distributors of industrial products. On the other hand, such products may be imported directly by U.S. manufacturers of processors.

U.S. manufacturing and processing firms have long constituted a major type of import purchaser for products of the developing countries. But these firms were basically buyers of the primary commodities, such as green coffee, copra, mineral ores, and crude petroleum. The purchase by industrial firms of large quantities of manufactured products is a relatively new phenomenon. To a certain extent, such imports are a reflection of the establishment of manufacturing subsidiaries in the developing countries by such large American or multinational firms as IBM, Ampex, Motorola, and Philco-Ford.[4] But it is likely that many of these imports represent purchases from independent suppliers in the developing countries.

Some light on the nature of the products purchased can be obtained from the recent U.S. Tariff Commission study on the use of Section 807 of the U.S. tariff schedules. This section provides duty exemption for American-made components of products assembled abroad. Table 17 lists some of the principal commodities involved in this trade. Note should be taken of the fact that the table covers only trade involving the assembly of American-made components. Nevertheless, it seems likely that the increase in this type of trade has been paralleled by an increase in imports of other types of manufactured products by industrial importers because of the development of these channels of distribution.

An exporter in a developing country can secure access to a substantial reservoir of information on the U.S. industrial market for manufactured imports. Detailed statistics on the value of shipments and the value added by manufacture of manufacturing establishments in all of the states and territories are compiled in the U.S. Census of Manufactures, taken most recently in 1967.[5] Statistics are reported in terms of some 400 categories of the U.S. four-digit Standard Industrial Classification (SIC), with product output statistics reported in more detailed seven-digit commodity classifications.[6] As a further assistance in locating producers of particular types of commodities, many directories of American manufacturers list the names and

TABLE 17

Principal Products Imported from
Less-Developed Countries
Under U.S. Tariff Section 807, 1969

Product	Value (million dollars)
Semiconductors and parts	87
TV receivers	40
Electronic memories	37
Other TV apparatus	30
Office machines and parts	30
Toys, dolls, and models	22
Radio apparatus and parts	17

Source: U.S. Tariff Commission, Economic Factors Affecting the Use of Items 807.00 and 806.30 of the Tariff Schedules of the United States, Investigation 332-61 (Washington, D.C.: U.S. Tariff Commission, September, 1970), Table 15, p. A-76.

addresses of producers by the four-digit SIC categories. Some of these directories concentrate on the larger companies;[7] others, produced by industrial-development agencies of individual states, attempt to list most or all of the firms within the borders of their State.[8]

The complexity and variety of U.S. industrial production complicates the identification of potential buyers for specific types of industrial products. For example, a foundry in a developing country may easily be able to identify all of the potential purchasers of its products in its own country. Table 18 both illustrates the greater complexity of this task in the United States market and suggests a manner in which it can be undertaken. The table shows over 100 purchasing "industries" for products of iron and steel foundries. In the input-output structure studies, the proportion of iron-and-steel-foundry products required for each dollar of output of each of the industries is also given.

MARKET SEGMENTATION

The 1970 achievement of a GNP of over 1 trillion dollars emphasizes the vast size of the American market. With a population of
over 200 million persons, a per capita GNP tremendously higher than
most of the developing countries, and a marketing area completely
contiguous except for Alaska, Hawaii, Puerto Rico, and the Virgin
Islands, the challenge presented to marketers who have not previously
sold to this market is perhaps somewhat intimidating.

The would-be supplier in the developing country may take com-
fort from the fact that even America's largest firms are compelled
to take various measures to segment this enormous market. In
advertising, for example, certain media, such as radio and television
stations and newspapers, provide an opportunity for matching expenditures to metropolitan areas. Because national magazines did not
originally furnish this capability, they found it necessary to acquire
it. Today, the largest American magazines offer complex printing
arrangements permitting advertising to be limited to one or a series
of special regional editions. Indeed, not even all of the largest firms
distribute throughout the United States market. A major oil company's
credit card is valid for six additional brands in order to give its users
national service. A major food product, although identically made,
must be advertised under different names in different parts of the
United States because of its separate marketing origins.

Table 19 shows U.S. customs districts with the largest duty collections and provides some indication of the major points at which
manufactured imports enter the U.S. market. Although the figures
shown are for duty collections, rather than the value of merchandise
entries, they are a good indication of the most important entry points
for manufactured goods, since primary products typically enter duty-
free or at modest rates of duty. These figures do not, however,
necessarily provide a good guide as to the location of American
importers. Mass-merchandising importers, for example, enter their
imports through the customs district most convenient to the regional
warehouse or outlet through which the products will be conveyed to
end-users. And even specialist importers do not enter imports
through the port at or near which they are located if this adds excessively to transportation costs. For example, New York importers of
oriental floor coverings presumably enter a good proportion of their
purchases intended for non-Eastern markets through West Coast
ports.

TABLE 18

Industries with Inputs from Iron-and-Steel-Foundries Industry
(input-output classification 3702; SIC 332)

Input-Output Industry		Related SIC Codes
Number	Title	(1957 editions)
	Mining	
9	Stone and clay mining and quarrying	
9.00	Stone and clay mining and quarrying	141, 142, 144, 145, 148, 149
10	Chemicals and fertilizer mineral mining	
10.00	Chemical and fertilizer mineral mining	147
	Construction	
11	New Construction	
11.02	New construction, nonresidential buildings	pt. 15, pt. 17
11.03	New construction, public utilities	pt. 15, pt. 16, pt. 17
11.04	New construction, highways	pt. 16, pt. 17
11.05	New construction, all other	pt. 15, pt. 16, pt. 17, 138
12	Maintenance and repair construction	
12.01	Maintenance and repair construction, residential buildings (nonfarm)	pt. 15, pt. 17
12.02	Maintenance and repair construction, all other	pt. 15, pt. 16, pt. 17
	Manufacturing	
13	Ordinance and accessories	
13.01	Complete guided missiles	1925
13.02	Ammunition, except for small arms, n.e.c.	1929
13.03	Tanks and tank components	1931
13.04	Sighting and fire control equipment	1941
13.05	Small arms	1951
13.07	Other ordinance and accessories	1911, 1999
24	Paper and allied products except containers and boxes	
24.07	Converted paper, products, n.e.c. except containers and boxes	2641, 2643, 2645, 2646, 2649
32	Rubber and miscellaneous plastics products	
32.03	Reclaimed rubber and miscellaneous rubber products, n.e.c.	3031, 3069
32.04	Miscellaneous plastics products	3079
35	Glass and glass products	
35.02	Glass containers	3221
36	Stone and clay products	

Input-Output Industry		Related SIC Codes (1957 edition)
Number	Title	
36.02	Brick and structural clay tile	3251
36.12	Ready-mixed concrete	3273
36.15	Cut stone and stone products	3281
36.16	Abrasive products	3291
37	Primary iron and steel manufacturing	
37.02	Iron and steel foundries	332
37.03	Iron and steel forgings	3391
37.04	Primary metal products, n.e.c.	3399
38	Primary nonferrous metals manufacturing	
38.07	Copper rolling and drawing	3351
38.08	Aluminum rolling and drawing	3352
38.09	Nonferrous rolling and drawing, n.e.c.	3356
38.11	Aluminum castings	3361
38.12	Brass, bronze and copper castings	3362
38.13	Nonferrous castings, n.e.c.	3369
40	Heating, plumbing and fabricated structural metal products	
40.01	Metal sanitary ware	3431
40.02	Plumbing fittings and brass goods	3432
40.03	Heating equipment except electric	3433
40.04	Fabricated structural steel	3441
40.05	Metal doors, sash and trim	3442
40.06	Fabricated plate work (boiler shops)	3443
40.07	Sheet metal work	3444
40.08	Architectural metal work	3446
40.09	Miscellaneous metal work	3449
41	Screw machine products, bolts, nuts, etc. and metal stampings	
41.01	Screw machine products and bolts, nuts, rivets and washers	345
41.02	Metal stampings	3461
42	Other fabricated metal products	
42.01	Cutlery	3421
42.02	Hand and edge tools including saws	3423, 3425
42.03	Hardware, n.e.c.	3429
42.05	Miscellaneous fabricated wire products	3481
42.07	Steel springs	3493
42.08	Pipe, valves, and pipe fittings	3494, 3498
42.11	Fabricated metal products, n.e.c.	3499

TABLE 18 (contd.)

Input-Output Industry		Related SIC Codes (1957 edition)
Number	Title	
	Manufacturing (cont.)	
43	Engines and turbines	
43.01	Steam engines and turbines	3511
43.02	Internal combustion engines, n.e.c.	3519
44	Farm machinery	
44.00	Farm machinery	3522
45	Construction, mining, oil-field machinery, equipment	
45.01	Construction machinery	3531
45.02	Mining machinery	3532
45.03	Oil-field machinery	3533
46	Materials handling machinery and equipment	
46.01	Elevators and moving stairways	3534
46.02	Conveyors and conveying equipment	3535
46.03	Hoists, cranes, and monorails	3536
46.04	Industrial trucks and tractors	3537
47	Metal working machinery and equipment	
47.01	Machine tools, metal-cutting types	3541
47.02	Machine tools, metal-forming types	3542
47.03	Special dies and tools and machine-tool accessories	3544, 3545
47.04	Metalworking machinery, n.e.c.	3548
48	Special industry machinery and equipment	
48.01	Food products machinery	3551
48.02	Textile machinery	3552
48.03	Woodworking machinery	3553
48.04	Paper industries machinery	3554
48.05	Printing-trades machinery	3555
48.06	Special industry machinery, n.e.c.	3559
49	General industrial machinery and equipment	
49.01	Pumps and compressors	3561
49.02	Ball and roller bearings	3562
49.03	Blowers and fans	3564
49.04	Industrial patterns	3565
49.05	Power transmission equipment	3566
49.07	General industrial machinery, n.e.c.	3569
50	Machine shop products	
50.00	Machine shop products	359

Input-Output Industry		Related SIC Codes (1957 edition)
Number	Title	
	Manufacturing (cont.)	
51	Office, computing, and accounting machines	
51.01	Computing and related machines	3571
51.02	Typewriters	3572
51.03	Scales and balances	3576
51.04	Office machines, n.e.c.	3579
52	Service industry machines	
52.01	Automatic merchandising machines	3581
52.02	Commercial laundry equipment	3582
52.03	Refrigeration machinery	3585
52.04	Measuring and dispensing pumps	3586
52.05	Service industry machines, n.e.c.	3589
53	Electric transmission and distribution equipment and electrical industrial apparatus	
53.01	Electric measuring instruments	3611
53.03	Switchgear and switchboard apparatus	3613
53.04	Motors and generators	3621
53.05	Industrial controls	3622
54	Household appliances	
54.01	Household cooking equipment	3631
54.02	Household refrigerators and freezers	3632
54.03	Household laundry equipment	3633
54.04	Electric housewares and fans	3634
54.05	Household vacuum cleaners	3635
54.06	Sewing machines	3636
54.07	Household appliances, n.e.c.	3639
55	Electric lighting and wiring equipment	
55.02	Lighting fixtures	3642
55.03	Wiring devices	3643, 3644
56	Radio, television, and communication equipment	
56.04	Radio and Television communication equipment	3662
57	Electronic components and accessories	
57.01	Electron tubes	3671, 3672, 3673
57.02	Semiconductors	3674
57.03	Electronic components, n.e.c.	3679

TABLE 18 (contd.)

Input-Output Industry		Related SIC Codes (1957 edition)
Number	Title	
	Manufacturing (cont.)	
58	Miscellaneous electrical machinery, equipment, and supplies	
58.03	X-ray apparatus and tubes	3693
58.04	Engine electrical equipment	3694
58.05	Electrical equipment, n.e.c.	3699
59	Motor vehicles and equipment	
59.01	Truck and bus bodies	3713
59.02	Truck trailers	3715
59.03	Motor vehicles and parts	3717
60	Aircraft and parts	
60.01	Aircraft	3721
60.02	Aircraft engines and parts	3722
60.03	Aircraft propellers and parts	3723
60.04	Aircraft equipment, n.e.c.	3729
61	Other transportation equipment	
61.01	Shipbuilding and repairing	3731
61.02	Boatbuilding and repairing	3732
61.03	Locomotives and parts	3741
61.04	Railroad and street cars	3742
61.05	Motorcycles, bicycles, and parts	3751
61.06	Trailer coaches	3791
61.07	Transportation equipment, n.e.c.	3799
62	Professional, scientific, and controlling instruments and supplies	
62.01	Engineering and scientific instruments	3811
62.02	Mechanical measuring devices	3821
62.03	Automatic temperature controls	3822
63	Optical, ophthalmic, and photographic equipment and supplies	
63.01	Optical instruments and lenses	3831
63.03	Photographic equipment and supplies	3861
64	Miscellaneous manufacturing	
64.03	Games, toys, etc.	3941
64.04	Sporting and athletic goods, n.e.c.	3949
	Transportation, Communication, Electric, Gas, and Sanitary Services	
65	Transportation and warehousing	
65.01	Railroads and related services	40, 474

Source: U.S., Department of Commerce, Office of Business Economics, Input-Output Structure of the U.S. Economy: 1963 (3 vols.; Washington, D.C.: U.S. Government Printing Office, 1969).

TABLE 19

U.S. Customs Districts
with Largest Aggregate Customs Duty Collections,
June 30, 1969

Customs District	Total Duty Collections (million dollars)
New York[a]	934
Los Angeles	225
Philadelphia	114
San Francisco	112
Chicago	103
Boston	83
Detroit	83
New Orleans	70
Baltimore	62
Seattle	54

[a]Regional office.

Source: U.S., Department of Treasury, Statistical Appendix to Annual Report, Secretary of the Treasury for the fiscal year ended June 30, 1969 (Washington: U.S. Government Printing Office, 1970), Table 13, pp. 54-55.

Some idea of the locations—in numbers, but not necessarily in size—of importers may be gained from an inspection of the Directory of United States Importers, a compilation by the Journal of Commerce of New York, which runs to over 700 pages.[9] The directory, which subdivides importers by their state of location, gives 38 percent of its listing pages to New York State (principal port: New York City). California (San Francisco and Los Angeles) receives another 13 percent. Illinois (Chicago) and New Jersey (Newark and Camden) each have about 5 percent; Pennsylvania (Philadelphia), North Carolina (Wilmington), Maryland (Baltimore), Massachusetts (Boston), Ohio

(Cleveland), and Texas (Houston) follow, each with about 3 percent. The states of Washington (Seattle), Florida (Miami), and Louisiana (New Orleans) each have about 2 percent of the listings, as does Puerto Rico. In all, more than three quarters of the listings are for only ten of the states.

The resources and abilities of the importer* must be determined both by investigation of the exporter in the developing country, and, hopefully, by a frank exchange of opinions between exporter and prospective importer. Some importers advise their suppliers that they do not attempt to cover more than a given portion of the American market; others assure their suppliers of their ability to tap the entire market. Thus, it behooves the exporter in the developing country to gain some idea of the location of his selling prospects in the American market.

One illustration may help to indicate how the best part of the American market for a given manufactured or processed export from a developing country can be reached without seeking to reach the entire geographical extent of the market. Imagine a fish sauce made in the Philippines that is a favorite food product in that country, but not very well known to persons without a Philippine background. According to the 1960 U.S. census, there were somewhat over 200,000 persons of Philippine origin in the country as of that year, 105,000 of whom had been born in the Philippines and the balance of Philippine or partially Philippine parentage.[10] These are obviously the prospects for the fish sauce. Where are they located? Further perusal of the census shows that 80,000 persons of Philippine origin were located in California, and the majority of these were living in two of the major metropolitan areas—27,000 in San Francisco-Oakland and 18,000 in Los Angeles-Long Beach.[11] Obviously, an importer with adequate distributive contacts in California should be able to reach what appears to be the greatest concentration of prospects for this product in the American market. Further research could turn up the facts about the balance of the Philippine population in the United States and assist in reaching some judgment as to what further distributive efforts, if any, are warranted in this case.

The preceding example is illustrative of the degree to which certain types of markets within the United States can be pinpointed. Various types of ethnic data can be used at different levels of significance: The piñata, a Mexican Christmas novelty, is probably also

---

*Dun and Bradstreet, Inc., of New York, is the largest organization in the United States furnishing financial and credit information on individual business firms.

popular to a certain degree among other Latin Americans, and data can be secured not only about the location of persons of Central American and South American origin, but also about all persons with a Spanish-language background.[12] Similarly, non-government research is available to locate the population professing various religious affiliations, a market indicator for a product like kosher-style foods.[13]

General types of market indicators—age group, sex, urban versus rural, etc.—are available for the approximately 3,000 counties or county equivalents into which the fifty U.S. states are subdivided. They are also available for what are known as Standard Metropolitan Statistical Areas (SMSAs). SMSAs are designations established by U.S. government agencies to delineate concentrations of population grouped about one or more cities and encompassing one or more counties, which coincide with wholesale distribution patterns and with such factors as the principal circulation area of major newspapers and the principal audience area of radio and television stations.[14]

For either county or metropolitan areas, various types of background data are available or physical conditions that may be important market indicators: general and seasonal climatic data such as average temperatures and humidities, range of elevations above sea-level, hardness of local water supplies, and so forth. Whether the manufactured product being exported from the developing country is a bathing suit or a water-softening appliance, such data may delimit the major marketing opportunities.

Income data are, of course, of major concern to all marketers. Two major sources of this type of data are the U.S. government's City and County Data Book and Sales Management magazine's "Survey of Buying Power."[15] In an effort to target the major "quality" markets, The New Yorker magazine has constructed a composite index of metropolitan areas designed to highlight those with the greatest purchasing power for products whose sales are highly correlated with high income.[16]

High-income consumers obviously do have greater degrees of optionality for their purchases (see Chapter 4), which makes them a particularly sought-after category for many marketers. The market for some types of products, however, tends to be negatively correlated with income levels; it is the low-income consumer who purchases such products as kerosene lamps and oil-fired space heaters. Other types of products, such as small room air conditioners, are doubtlessly purchased in the greatest numbers primarily by middle-income consumers.

The construction of a marketing profile for a particular manufactured export from the developing country may be a task beyond
the capabilities of the supplier. Yet, an awareness of the marketing
factors within the United States may serve two general purposes.
First, it may help to convince the supplier that the particular submarket
for his products in the United States is limited enough and locatable
enough to make export possible; second, it can enable him more intel-
ligently to deal with an American importer, or several importers, in
working out a distribution plan for tapping the American market. The
execution of this plan must be left in the hands of the importers, but
an informed awareness by the supplier can aid immeasurably in the
success of the supplier-importer marketing partnership.

EXCLUSIVITY

A perennial problem in the marketing of manufactured goods is
the degree of exclusivity to be given to distributors. To the extent
that a supplier is striving for the greatest possible aggregate sales
volume, he is tempted to sell to the greatest possible number of distributors. In the case of certain types of well-advertised and long-
promoted products, where the end-user literally tends to demand the
items wherever he goes (e.g., America's major soft drinks), the policy
of maximizing the number of distributive outlets is obviously sound.
For most sellers, however, there is an inescapable formula: the
amount of promotional effort that a distributor is willing to put behind
an individual product varies inversely with the number of other firms
that are distributing the product in his area.[17]

Again, the problem can often be solved by marketers where
there are fairly clear-cut regional lines observed by distributors.
To return to the soft drink example, but at the bottling level, shipping
costs tend to limit bottlers to relatively confined geographic areas,
and a New York bottler is unlikely to try to absorb the freight costs
of shipping bottled drinks from New York into say, the Cleveland
market. But this question may be more complex in the case of imports
that may enter the U.S. market from different ports. Will selection
of separate importers in Miami, New Orleans, Los Angeles, and Seattle
decrease the effort of a New York importer? This depends on whether
he considers himself to be serving the other areas named. As mentioned previously, some importers advise their supplier that they
cannot adequately tap the American market in areas far from their
place of business; others may be in a position to assure him that
they can do a national selling job for him in the American market.

It is easy, nonetheless, to pinpoint certain things that an exporter of manufactured products in the developing countries should not do in his American distribution. Several importers contacted by the writer (BA, BL, BW) complained that their suppliers had no concept of limited distribution, but simply responded to any and all inquiries from the United States with price quotations. Such quotations break two rules normally observed in distribution in the U.S. market: they invade the regional market that the importer-distributor may have reason to assume was offered exclusively to him and they tend to disregard differences in the level of distribution.

PRICING MARGINS

Most manufactured goods—particularly consumer products— tend to have a formal pricing structure in the American market. The price to the end-user is typically represented in a list price, and prices to wholesale buyers are stated as discounts from this list price.[18]

Except for automobiles, for which specific federal legislation was enacted requiring the labeling of list prices, and products for which prices are established under state "fair trade" legislation, list prices may be only a point of departure for the quotation of actual prices even to the end-user.[19] Sellers of industrial-type products, for example, may expect most buyers to pay a net price substantially under their own published list prices. Most sellers, however, also tend to have a fairly firm idea of the discounts at which they offer their products to distributors who resell. For consumer-type products, for example, the most typical resellers are likely to be wholesalers who sell to retailers and retailers who sell to household consumers.

Under the Robinson-Patman Act, differences in price (or price- affecting allowances) are considered nondiscriminatory if justified by differences in cost.[20] Suppliers generally try to tie price differences, accordingly, to quantity-related cost differences. Obviously, the larger the unit of purchase, the more economical the cost of distribu- tion per unit is likely to be. Some functions, such as invoicing, are basically the same for either large or small orders; other functions, such as packing, can be more economically performed for larger orders.

Notwithstanding the sometimes controversial specifics of pricing margins, the exporter who sells to different levels of distribution at the same price is violating a basic custom of the market—that margins are supposed to be arranged in such a way that each purchaser can secure the most advantageous price from the firm that normally would be expected to sell him. Thus, American marketers would not expect a supplier in Korea, for example, to sell wigs to a retail store, which may order a dozen or less, at the same price that he sells to a distributor who orders by the hundreds; nor would they expect him to quote the same price that he quotes to a retail store to an individual who wants to buy a wig for personal use. Yet, numerous instances were reported in which this apparently simple rule of good marketing was disregarded (importers AY, BA, BC).

THE ROLE OF SALES PROMOTION IN DISTRIBUTION

Unquestionably, the American mass-consumption economic engine is fueled by large expenditures for sales promotion. The most evident indication of this is the size of U.S. annual expenditures for advertising and related activities. It is estimated that such expenditures in 1969 were in excess of $19.5 billion, with almost $6 billion of this represented by newspaper advertising, over $3.5 billion by television advertising, over $2.5 billion for the cost of direct mail advertising, and radio and magazines together accounting for another $2.5 billion.[21] Indicative of the pervasiveness of sales promotion as a way of economic life in the United States is the fact that over 40 percent of the estimated $19.5-billion total represented expenditures by local firms—wholesalers and retailers—as distinguished from the expenditures by the owners of national brands.

But even the foregoing figures do not give a full picture of the importance of sales promotion in U.S. distribution. They do not include the cost of sales promotion via "point of sale displays" and personal selling. They do not include the investments in deals designed to promote sales by offering combination prices, premiums, contests, etc., or such miscellaneous techniques as trade shows, product publicity stories placed in the news columns of newspapers and magazines, and so forth.[22] All of this is evidence of the American preference for moving the demand curve to the right through demand-influencing activities, rather than attempting to increase sales simply through price reductions (see the discussion in Chapter 3).

It is true that some of the most intensive promotional efforts—as evidenced by the size of national advertising budgets—are for limited categories of consumer goods, such as cigarettes, detergents, proprietary remedies, and automobiles.[23] It is also true that products distributed by the mass merchandisers under brand names chosen by them are promoted by the mass merchandisers themselves. Nonetheless, the promotional decisions for thousands of products on the American market are made by the prime suppliers of such products, who, in the case of domestically made products, are the manufacturers. Who takes the responsibility in the case of imported products?

It has already been noted (Chapter 4) that there are leading trademarks on the American market for such well-known imports as Rolls Royce automobiles and Sony electronic equipment. Obviously, in cases such as these, the foreign supplier must at least share in the promotional decisions made for marketing the products in the United States. But with few exceptions—a liquor importer (AW) would like some promotional assistance and a department store (BS) believes it might be helpful—all of the importers contacted in this study who commented on the matter felt certain that promotion had to be the responsibility of the U.S. importer.[24] Some importers went further, stating that this applied not only to manufactured imports from the developing countries, but to imports from such established sources as Western Europe.

In general, the reason cited by importers for assuming this responsibility was the lack of knowledge on the part of foreign suppliers of the techniques of sales promotion in the United States. This was not considered to be a hindrance to the sale of such products in the U.S. market; instead, importers indicated a complete willingness to shoulder the promotional responsibility, asking only that their cost price be low enough to discharge this function. In one instance, an importer (AE) indicated that a willingness to understand the problems of competitive sales promotion in the United States might include an acceptance by an exporter in the developing country of a lower price when demand problems called for more intensive promotion. Hopefully, the importer felt, such price reductions might be counterbalanced by higher prices for other products easier to promote. There was, incidentally, no call by importers for promotional efforts by foreign suppliers to reach them. The importer apparently is wary of such efforts as unsolicited mailings. Said one importer (BA), "Business, primarily, has to be done by sampling rather than by printed material."

The emphasis on securing a price low enough to perform promotional functions should not be interpreted as a heedless quest for price reductions on the part of importers. The very act of sales promotion implies an investment not only in immediate sales, but in future sales prospects, and thus requires a continuing dependable source of supply. In one case, the supplier's efforts to furnish the product at a low price were counter-productive to the goal of dependability.

Case History CB-1

The product was decorative (crystal) glassware. The importer (CB) was contacted by a supplier in a South Asian country that had not previously entered the U.S. market. He was asked, and he advised his new supplier, what a desirable price level would be. Initial shipments were made at that price, and the product was quite salable. The supplier, however, had apparently not considered his own cost level in agreeing to the price and apparently found himself unable economically to continue shipments profitably. Although the importer tried to offer a higher price to secure continuation of the supply, the loss experienced by his supplier apparently dissuaded further efforts at export.

SUMMARY

In this chapter, the problems of achieving an adequate distribution system for conveying manufactured imports from the developing-country supplier to the American end-user have been discussed. Differentiations have been drawn between the specialist importer and the mass-merchandising importer. In general, the specialist appears to cater to a more limited and unique type of demand, while the mass-merchandiser's concerns are middle of the road. In some cases, the exporter in the developing country may begin by selling to the specialist importer and later achieve the resources necessary to secure the large-quantity orders of the mass-merchandising importer, as well as meeting his other requirements, such as those of exact timing of supply.

Details have been presented indicating the increasing importance of industrial firms as importers of manufactured products from the developing countries. Substantial informational resources are available for the identification of prospects in this market.

The enormous size of the U.S. market has been found to have had an impact on the marketing activities of even the largest U.S. firms. Certain clues as to the concentration of importers and import traffic volume have been presented, but is suggested that a marketing plan will depend primarily upon the methods and resources of the importer or importers involved in the distribution of the product from the developing country. Proposals are made to aid the exporter in understanding the demand profile for his product in the United States.

Exclusive sales rights have been identified as a matter of particular concern to distributors of imported manufactured products from the developing countries. Apparently, many suppliers in these countries offer to sell their products freely to any would-be purchasers and fail to understand the differing price levels in the American market for different levels of distribution. Respect for both of these normal features of marketing in the United States might be extremely helpful in the improvement of distribution of the manufactured imports involved.

Finally, the importance of sales promotion in American marketing has been described. The consensus of the firms importing manufactured products from the developing countries appears to be that the sales-promotion task has to be left to the U.S. firms. The supplier's role has been depicted as furnishing the product at a price that makes possible the performance of the promotional function by U.S. distributors. The price, however, must not be so low as to interfere with the supply.

NOTES

1. The definition of the term "channels of distribution" through which this is accomplished has not been a matter of agreement among marketing experts. A review of varying definitions is presented by William Davidson in Lee Adler, ed., Plotting Marketing Strategy (New York: Simon and Schuster, 1967), pp. 261-63. Mr. Davidson proposes defining the channel of distribution as "the course taken in the transfer of title to a commodity," but some types of distributors, including importers, act as agents and perform distributive functions without actually taking legal title to the products involved.

2. Alfred Oxenfeldt, Executive Action in Marketing (Belmont, Calif.: Wadsworth Publishing Co., 1966), p. 433, discusses this matter as follows: "Can we say, again relying on common sense, that the fewer the layers of resellers involved, the more efficient the distribution system? Again, one would be mistaken to agree. By introducing an additional middleman, a manufacturer may gain access to a much broader market. For example, the middleman may currently deal with precisely the distributors that the manufacturer desires for his product. The costs of trying to win those distributors to his distribution system might be much larger than middleman costs."

3. A discussion, for non-Americans, of the purchasing and sales operations of American mass-merchandisers such as Gimbel's, Macy's, and Sears Roebuck appears in Distribution des Biens de

Consommation en Amérique du Nord (Paris: Comité Franc-Dollar, October, 1967).

    4. New York Times, January 3, 1971, p. 12F, col. 2.

    5. See U.S., Bureau of the Census, Publication Program, 1967 Census of Manufactures and Mineral Industries, No. 4 (Washington, D.C., January, 1970.

    6. See "Industry Classification of Establishments," in U.S., Bureau of the Census, 1967 Census of Manufacturers: Grain Mill Products, MC67(20)-20D (Washington, D.C.: U.S. Government Printing Office, 1970), pp. v-vi.

    7. For example, Dun and Bradstreet, Million Dollar Directory, 1970 (New York, 1970); and Dun and Bradstreet, Middle Market Directory, 1971 (New York, 1970).

    8. Examples of directories that use SIC designations include: 1968 California Manufacturers Directory (Los Angeles: Times Mirror Press, 1968); Missouri Directory of Manufacturers, (1966 ed., Jefferson City: Missouri Division of Commercial and Industrial Development, 1968); 1967 Annual New Jersey State Industrial Directory (New York, 1962); Directory of Ohio Manufacturers, 1961 (Columbus: State of Ohio Department of Industrial Relations, 1961); and Directory of Texas Manufacturers, 1962 (Austin: University of Texas Bureau of Business Research, 1962).

    9. Journal of Commerce, Directory of United States Importers (1969 ed., New York: Twin Coast Newspapers, Inc., 1968).

    10. U.S. Bureau of the Census, U.S. Census of Population: 1960. Detailed Characteristics, U.S. Summary PC(1)-ID (Washington, D.C.: U.S. Government Printing Office, 1963), Table 162, p. 1-366

    11. U.S., Bureau of the Census, U.S. Census of Population: 1960. Detailed Characteristics, California PC(1)-6D. (Washington, D.C.: U.S. Government Printing Office, 1962), Table 99, p. 6-492.

    12. U.S., Bureau of the Census, U.S. Census of Population, 1960. Subject Reports: Persons of Spanish Surname PG(2)-B (Washington, D.C.: U.S. Government Printing Office, 1963).

    13. National Council of the Churches of Christ in the U.S.A., Yearbook of American Churches for 1969. See World Almanac, 1969 (New York: Newspaper Enterprise Association, 1968), pp. 219-20.

14. See U.S., Bureau of the Census, City and County Data Book 1967 (Washington, D.C.: U.S. Government Printing Office, 1967), pp. xiii and xiv.

15. Sales Management magazine publishes an "Annual Survey of Buying Power." The 39th such survey was published as the magazine's June 10, 1968, issue. The survey includes city, county, and metropolitan area data on population and retail sales (total and major categories), as well as "sales activity" and "buying power" indexes.

16. See "United States Primary Markets for Quality Merchandise," International Trade Forum, June, 1967, pp. 29-31.

17. The intensity of distributive effort has been correlated with the number of distributive outlets. At one extreme, intensive distribution (the use of a large number of distributors) has been correlated with minimum marketing effort by each distributor; at the other, exclusive distribution is correlated with maximum marketing effort. G. A. Field, J. Douglas, and L.X. Tarpey, Marketing Management: A Behavioral Systems Approach (Columbus, Ohio: Merrill Books, Inc., 1966), pp. 424-25.

18. Trade discount structures are described in S. H. Rewoldt, J. D. Scott, and M. R. Warshaw, Introduction to Marketing Management (Homewood, Ill.: R. D. Irwin, 1969), pp. 553-55. For a discussion of pricing structures for industrial goods, and manufacturers' attitudes on resulting distributor margins, see William Diamond, Distribution Channels for Industrial Goods, Monograph 114 (Colombus: Ohio State University, Bureau of Business Research, 1963), pp. 135-44.

19. The so-called fair-trade laws of some of the states authorize manufacturers to establish mandatory minimum resale prices for their products, and federal legislation authorizes such arrangements between such states. Restrictive judicial interpretation of such laws, however, has contributed to the decline of this practice. See B. S. Yamey "Resale Price Maintenance," in the International Encyclopedia of the Social Sciences (New York: Macmillan Company and Free Press, 1968). Vol. XIII, pp. 479-82.

20. Public Law 692, 74th Congress (1936) amended by Public Law 550, 75th Congress (1938). The law prohibits "any person . . . to discriminate in price between different purchasers . . . where the effect . . . may be substantially to lessen competition . . ." (Section 2[a]). See Nathan Baily, ed., Marketing Profitably Under the Robinson-Patman Act (Washington, D.C.: Public Affairs Press, 1963). Also, U.S., Federal Trade Commission, Guides for Advertising Allowances

and Other Merchandising Payments and Services (Washington, D.C., 1969).

21. Marketing/Communications, February, 1970, pp. 54-55.

22. Both European and U.S. consumer goods companies are considered to be devoting increasing funds to such "below the line" promotion techniques. International Trade Forum, February, 1970, pp. 4-8, 44-45.

23. See "Top 125 National Advertisers of 1969," Advertising Age, July 13, 1970, p. 37.

24. A research team for the GATT/UNCTAD International Trade Center concluded that a small investment by producers of oriental carpets would be worthwhile as a means of influencing demand in the consuming countries. International Trade Forum, July, 1970, p. 15.

8

THE
COMMUNICATION PROBLEM
AND
EXPORTER DEPENDABILITY

THE EXPORTER-IMPORTER RELATIONSHIP

The relationship of the American importer and his supplier or would-be supplier in the developing country has been examined in various aspects in the preceding chapters. Chapter 3 discussed the importance of the importer's selection of supplier; subsequent chapters discussed such issues as the production of designs suitable for the American market, the volition to establish and hold adequate quality levels, the concern about satisfactory packaging, and attention to the details of distribution. "Dependability" might be the word an importer would use to cover such matters. All of these questions were seen to be marketing issues that can, at least in part, be dealt with by developing-country suppliers. Yet, the testimony of American importers shows that these matters were frequently disregarded or neglected. It is the purpose of this chapter to examine the causes of this apparent shortcoming, with a view to determining ways in which it can be remedied.

One incidental issue is treated first: do suppliers of manufactured products in developing countries have the ability to cope with such technicalities as documentation, insurance, and shipping, or are these a hindrance to the expansion of their shipments into the U.S. market?

The chapter then examines the nature of the communication problem between exporters and importers to shed light on the degree to which this may explain the apparent failure of exporters to serve importers in the aspects of marketing discussed above. The communication problem is first examined in its most obvious—linguistic—setting, but then probed more deeply in an attempt to determine the extent to which communication difficulties are matters of cultural or even philosophical differences.

Following this, the chapter discusses the reactions of importers to what they have experienced in the way of communication difficulties. To the extent that such difficulties can be alleviated, the entire exporter-importer relationship presumably can be improved, with consequent benefit in all of the aspects treated in the preceding chapters.

THE TECHNICALITIES OF TRADE

Economists have long emphasized imperfections in the competitive process stemming from difficulties of entry: many industries, in their opinion, were imperfectly competitive because new firms could enter the field only with considerable difficulty, if at all. Traditionally, the main obstacle to entry has been identified as the magnitude of capital resources required. More recently, however, it has become increasingly clear that lack of knowledge can be a substantial barrier to entry.[1] A company desiring to initiate the manufacture of lasers, for example, would have to marshall considerable manufacturing information before it could go into production. Conversely, groups of experts in scientific fields such as lasers have been able to found their own companies because their know-how made the proposed venture attractive enough to others who possessed the requisite capital. Accordingly, it is appropriate to ask whether the lack of knowledge of the technicalities of international trade furnishes a barrier to the entry of additional firms as suppliers of manufactured imports from the developing countries.

There are, after all, considerable complexities to international trade in such matters as export documentation, shipping arrangements, and insurance. The special problems of packing have already been discussed in Chapter 6. But to indicate just a few of the additional complications, the act of export itself sometimes requires the completion of complex official forms in developing countries. Then the shipper of a manufactured export must not only select a carrier or carriers to be used, but must reserve the necessary space (sometimes a complex matter, as in the case of perishable or highly valuable cargo), determine that he is paying no more than the most favorable rate available, and prepare the appropriate bill of lading. He must assure himself that his insurance coverage is best suited for his purposes and know what to do in the event of a claim.[2] Similar questions are posed in the handling of traditional (primary-commodity) exports, but, as was pointed out in Chapter 6, the arrangements for these products are fairly well standardized.

It is not surprising that against this background the opinion has been expressed that technicalities furnish a formidable barrier against expansion of the exports of manufactured goods from the developing countries.[3] Surprisingly, however, this opinion was not reflected in the comments of most of the importers contacted during the course of this study. Of the twenty-eight firms that expressed an opinion on this matter, only one seemed to feel that this constituted a substantial barrier to entry of new firms into the supply. Three types of comments did appear:

1. The lack of knowledge of some suppliers in these matters can cause an additional cost in these transactions, and gaining greater expertise is an important ingredient in the development of successful trade relationships (importers AY, AZ, BW)

2. The use of an export agent or exporter is particularly advisable in the case of small or smaller manufacturing firms in the developing countries (importers AA, AB, AK, AZ, BD, BL)

3. In any event, it is a fundamental responsibility of the importer to help his supplier in any way that he can (importers AD, AW, AY, BC, BW, BZ).

A general optimism on the part of American importers concerning the ability of new suppliers to cope with the technicalities of trade was expressed in comments such as the following: "Traders can be found who will do all of this" (AA); "A good American importer can give his assistance" (AD); "If the product that is wanted [can be found] at the right price, someone can be found to do the rest of the work" (AJ); "Small factories can always use shipping agents" (AK); "Our experience has indicated that most countries have people experienced in shipping, insurance and documentation" (BQ); and "Minor problem once selling initiated. They'd make it a point to learn" (BS). There was some indication that one of the problems in handling the technicalities of exporting was the very efforts of governments in the developing countries to assist in promoting exports.

Many developing countries have complex export-promotion schemes. Some of these work through the mechanisms used to control the allocation of foreign exchange. Although the programs concentrate on the provision of incentives to export, they apparently can become so complicated that some supplier firms find themselves more involved in trading rights to foreign exchange than export commodities. In cases such as these, the export-promotion programs of the governments may actually become a hindrance to export rather than an incentive (importer BX and exporter PB).[4]

THE COMMUNICATION PROBLEM

Communication—the transmission of information and ideas (particularly instructions) between individuals—is of the same critical importance to business activities as it is to social relationships. Within an organization and between organizations, the degree of effectiveness of communication may dictate the success or failure of the undertaking.

Men have communicated with one another since before the dawn of history without, until recently, attempting to elevate this basic fact of human relationships to the status of a science. Yet, this in no way diminishes the importance of the field nor its requirement for urgent attention in the business world.[5] Using the most general terms, communication may be said to be practiced in two ways: face to face and remotely, either by speech (telephone) or in writing. Since this study deals with trading relationships, mass communication—newspapers, television, etc.—is not considered, although in the form of advertising such communication is one of the most important forces in the American market.

Face-to-face communication is generally considered to be more effective than remote communication with one important exception: unless some device like a tape recorder is used, there is no record of any spoken communication to refer back to subsequently. It is for this reason that American business firms frequently state on their memorandum forms such comments as, "Write it—don't say it." Obviously, the person receiving a written communication can refer to it as frequently as needed, and no dispute should later arise between the parties as to what was the substance of the instruction.

So it would seem, at any rate. But, actually, the written instruction minus the gestures, expressions, inflections, tone of voice, pronunication, emphasis, etc., of a verbal instruction is much more abbreviated in its content. More important, the spoken instruction—and this applies to a reasonable extent to remote instruction given by telephone—permits feedback to the person giving the instruction. If he notes that the listener obviously is distracted by something else, he will realize that the instruction must be repeated. If the listener responds in a way that indicates his misinterpretation of the instruction, the instructor can try to clarify the meaning. Both spoken and written instructions suffer from the fact that they must utilize words. Justice Oliver Wendell Holmes' comment on the shortcomings of words is still as apt as when it was made over fifty years ago: "A word is not a crystal, transparent and unchanged; it is the skin of a living thing and may vary greatly in color and content according to the circumstances and the time in which it is used."[6]

An additional special problem of business communication is that a message is seldom received in isolation. Usually, it follows a series of previous contacts. If a businessman sends another businessman an order for stove bolts after having previously alerted the second businessman to expect an order for wood screws, the recipient of the order must resolve the apparent contradiction in the communications he has received. Experiments at the Foundation for Research on Human Behavior indicate that the recipient, if he cannot directly question the conflicting information, will use various means to try to force it to agree with previously secured information.[7] And the results of such conflicts are frequently an erroneous handling of the order. The smaller businessman is particularly beset with communication problems. A U.S. study of small business firms commented:

> The over-all picture presented in this study of the small
> businessman with reference to his use of information is
> generally one of inadequacy. He makes inadequate use of
> the information available; he has inadequate knowledge of
> his own problems; he has inadequate knowledge of the in-
> formation which might assist him in the solution of his
> problems . . . .[8]

All of the preceding communication problems seem to have been designed to plague particularly international trade. Face-to-face communication is expensive and must be limited; written communication problems are accentuated by the fact that many must be by cable, where the need for brevity means that the drawbacks of such communication are greatly increased. And finally, in developing new sources of manufactured imports from the developing countries, small businessmen must, at least initially, be largely involved.

Yet, all of these considerations are perhaps only precursors to persons' of different nationalities doing business with one another.[9] The reflections of these differences can be dealt with on two levels: language and culture. It would be appropriate to point out at this juncture that most of the problems discussed in this section apply, with varying degrees of intensity, to all international business relations and particularly to all international trade relations. As Chapter 2 demonstrated, this has not prevented a tremendous expansion of such trade.

The reason, nonetheless, for treating these problems in detail in this study is that here a new type of trade is being discussed, in which people who have not traded before products that have not been importantly involved in trade before are concerned. The effort required to institute this type of trade is of a completely different order from that required to continue or intensify trade between developed countries or between the United States and the developing countries in primary commodities. As one importer (BN) of manufactured products put it, "The distance from Japan to Korea can be the distance (in our business) from Trenton to the moon."

The problems of dealing in different languages should not be dismissed as simply a problem of interpretation and translation. Unless the businessman chiefly responsible for the transaction involved is bilingual himself—in the language as it is spoken in the country with which he is dealing, e.g., Argentinian Spanish or Moroccan French—the conveyance of ideas and information from one language to another opens up great possibilities for misinterpretation or error.[10]

In theory, at least, developing countries with Anglo-American historical backgrounds may have an advantage over others in that more of the businessmen are likely to speak English. Thus, the Philippines, India, and many of the Caribbean countries may have one less communication problem to cope with than, say, South American countries or African countries that were formerly French colonies. Yet, when negotiations are conducted in English, the danger of misinterpretation, though less apparent, may be even greater than when other languages are involved. The Englishman who says, "I got a flat last night," may mean that he rented an apartment; the American, using the same words, may mean that the tire of his automobile was punctured. The discrepancies of meaning in English can be much greater where a developing country is concerned.[11] In the Philippines, residents of Manila proudly refer to their first public housing project as a "tenement"; the American Heritage Dictionary offers this definition of the word: "A run-down low-rental apartment building or rooming house whose facilities and maintenance barely meet minimum standards." Obviously, no American would be proud of a building referred to as a "tenement."

A hazard in all communication, and particularly in communication between persons of different nationalities, is the use of stereotypes.

Until and unless people become very well acquainted with one another, they tend to judge each other in terms of stereotypes. In the same country, stereotypes may be triggered by last names, sex, manner of dress and speech, physical appearance, etc.[12] Between countries, many people have been conditioned to ascribe certain national characteristics to one another. Stereotypes can actually interfere with the substance of communication to the extent that the recipient disregards the words of an instruction and substitutes what he assumes a person of his chosen stereotype really is saying. This is perhaps reminiscent of the writer's absent-minded friend who would offer an acquaintance a cigarette and then, forgetting that it was refused, hold a match under the acquaintance's nose to light the cigarette that wasn't there!

Writers frequently emphasize cultural differences, of which linguistic differences are only a part, in discussing barriers to international business. The external manifestations are easy to perceive: the Japanese bows rather than shaking hands with his associates; the Latin stands right next to the person he is addressing; Americans frequently entertain their business associates in their homes, while businessmen of other nationalities rarely if ever do so.

But these externalities are not as serious a barrier to international business as certain alleged differences in basic business philosophy. American businessmen, for example, like to think of themselves as committed to long-range profits (and, therefore, reinvestment and growth). The charge is frequently leveled at businessmen of other countries, particularly of the developing countries, that short-range profits are the only real interest of their operations. Put another way, it is alleged that many businessmen in the developing countries demand rewards for minor risk-taking far beyond those Americans think appropriate. Also, it is claimed that many businessmen stay away from such areas as manufacturing and export of manufactured goods because they feel the rewards cannot compensate for the degree of risk involved and that they limit their endeavors instead to real estate speculation or to traditional types of primary-products export.[13]

It is worth noting, parenthetically, that governments of many of the developing countries appear to campaign for the virtual elimination of profits. Competition of public enterprise with private enterprise, proposals for the elimination of patents and strict control over foreign licensing schemes, and pressure against the repatriation of foreign investments may all be interpreted as opposition to the profit system.[14] Accordingly, exporters or would-be exporters of

manufactured goods from some of these countries may be accused
of excessively short-run attitudes toward profit-making at the same
time that their governments may seem bent on the elimination of
profits. The two apparently opposite trends may, unfortunately, be
consistent with one another, to the detriment of expanded manufactured
exports.

A further criticism has been leveled against the philosophy of
businessmen in the developing countries: that those involved in manufacturing live in sheltered markets and accordingly are not philosoph-
ically equipped to cope with the intense level of competition in world
export markets for their products (see the comments in Chapter 5
on the reflection of this factor in the quality issue). The traveler in
developing countries is exposed to this high price-low quality equation
time and again in local market places. It is obvious that overcoming
this handicap, at least in part, will require some dualism, in that producers who serve both domestic and export markets must gear their
production and pricing policies to different targets. Unfortunately,
this is not practical in all cases.

An illustration of the problems of communication is the matter
of delivery on time. Delivery, after all, represents the culmination
of all of the supplier's efforts: his production of the articles wanted
in the quantities offered and his selection and use of the transportation agencies necessary to convey the products to their destination
by the target date.* Beset by these difficulties, it is obvious that a
supplier who is not completely convinced of the urgent necessity of
delivery by the target date is almost certain not to meet this requirement. While buyers may seek punitive actions for late delivery, it
is a business axiom that penalties are never equivalent to lost sales
opportunities. No importer can continue in business in the face of
consistent failure of his suppliers to deliver as promised.

---

*The difficulty of two-way communication in international trading
also handicaps the exporter who complies with instructions furnished
by the importer, but knows that better arrangements could be made.
Exporter PA cites the instance when a vessel is specified by the importer, and this vessel is delayed. The exporter might be able to
suggest a faster alternate sailing, but is handicapped by the difficulty
of communicating with the importer.

IMPORTER REACTIONS TO
THE COMMUNICATION PROBLEM

Importers contacted during the study alluded frequently to the communication problem. In some cases, these allusions referred to what might be deemed relatively minor failures of communication; in others, to what appeared to be basic differences in business outlook and philosophy, although one importer (AS) criticized other American importers for what he considered short-sighted, quick-profit attitudes of the type sometimes attributed to firms in developing countries. There is, however, reason to hope that communication short-falls will become less important in the future. Perhaps the greatest re-assurance is furnished by the statistics in Chapter 2 which indicate that manufactured imports from the developing countries have been increasing. Doubtlessly, the demonstration effect can be counted on to attract additional firms into this type of trade.

In addition, certain suppositions may be made concerning the creation of additional entrepreneurial resources in the developing countries.[15] For one thing, international firms have been under continuing pressure in most countries to train local nationals for positions of responsibility in their operations. These individuals do not always remain in the firms that trained them, but may branch out into other local enterprises and use their international training to promote manufactured exports. Another factor has been the popularity of American graduate business schools as a training ground for individuals from the developing countries. One writer theorizes that what is really transmitted through these schools, when their training is successful, is the American entrepreneurial outlook—with its long-range and risk-taking ideals—rather than just the details of administrative knowledge.[16]

The general optimism referred to earlier in the chapter was reflected also in the opinions of importers as to what might be done about the communication problem. To begin with, importers try to cope with the communication problem by traveling to the countries from which they buy. This substitutes face-to-face contact with their sources for written contacts, at least at one stage. Mass-merchandisers who maintain buying offices have a continuing channel through which face-to-face contact can be used to supplement written communications. Other importers (AE and BW) suggested that suppliers be exposed to the American business environment in situ.

Some importers felt that the instructions for product design, quality, packaging, and delivery could only really be understood by their suppliers if they could see the products on the shelves of the American stores or elsewhere passing through the American market place. In many of the countries where small outlets bargaining with limited quantities of goods are still the fundamental fact of commerce, the importers were convinced that the American scene had to be viewed to be believed. Although such a remedy to their communication problems might seem overly simplistic, one importer (BW) had actually had experience with visits of suppliers from the developing countries and felt that the wisdom of this suggestion had been demonstrated in such instances.

Proposals for bringing exporters or suppliers from developing countries to the United States to see the American distribution system at work may seem at least partly superfluous in view of the growing penetration into their own countries of certain aspects of the American system. The pioneering work in Venezuela of the International Basic Economy Corporation (IBEC) in introducing the supermarket to that country is fairly well known.[17] Manila now has several very up-to-date supermarkets, and one of the key figures in establishing several of those supermarkets is reportedly working on a similar development for Singapore.[18] In other countries, such as Mexico, the supermarket is no longer a novelty.[19]

Yet, presumably importers do not feel that the incursion of a limited degree of modern merchandising into the developing countries is a sufficient demonstration of the American mass-merchandising scene. Such supermarkets still generally represent a special situation in most of the developing countries, whose predominant distribution system remain traditional. This is inevitable, since the American economy is one of mass consumption, and the characteristics that make it so will not be duplicated in the developing countries until they, too, become mass-consumption economies.

INTERNATIONAL CLEARINGHOUSE
FOR NEW IMPORTS

During the course of this study, a suggestion made by one of the importers (AT) appeared to uncover a major gap in the communication channels between importers and suppliers or would-be suppliers in the developing countries. The importer suggested that some type of international clearinghouse be established through which new products could be exposed to potential distributors. The products under discussion were, of course, manufactured exports from the developing countries, and the recipient countries might be either industrialized or developing countries. The suggestion, however, was examined in terms of its possible applicability to the United States.

This is of particular importance. Developing countries have sometimes shown an apparently greater willingness to seek market opportunities in other developing countries or in industrialized countries other than the United States because of their hesitancy in tackling what appears to them to be too formidable a marketing objective—the American market.[20]

The writer developed that suggestion, in discussions with other importers, along the following lines. An international clearinghouse established under noncommercial auspices, such as within the GATT/UNCTAD International Trade Center, would receive offers to supply new types of manufactured exports and relay them to importers (e.g., in the United States). Such products would be new in that the company offering to supply them would not have supplied them to any distributor in the country being contacted—the clearinghouse would never accept a proposal when the supplier's purpose was only to gain a new distributor to replace one he already had in a particular country. The proposals might be backed up with some on-the-spot verification by either the clearinghouse or another noncommercial agency, such as the United Nations Industrial Development Organization (UNIDO).

The general reaction of importers was that such an operation could greatly supplement their existing efforts to locate new sources. Per contra, as mentioned in Chapter 7, they are generally resistant to unsolicited mailings that come to many of them with apparent frequency; in one case (See Chapter 4), the export-promotion efforts of the Korean consulate in New York figured favorably. But the clearinghouse, presumably applying to all developing countries and presumably imposing some reasonably selective regimen on suppliers using it, would apparently open up new lines of opportunity for expanding an importer's sources of manufactured goods.

Among the twenty-four importers queried on the subject of the clearinghouse, twenty were favorable. Three (AH, CC, CH) of the remaining four did not wish to expand their sources of supply (their areas of specialization were narrow, or the supplying country was traditionally associated with their product). The fourth (CK) felt that his products were too sophisticated for any developing country to supply (see the discussion in Chapter 1). This generally favorable reaction to the clearinghouse proposal appears to indicate that a gap in the communication process (the selection of new sources) has been identified. Although the importance of this gap or the results that could be achieved by attempting to close it in the manner suggested (an international clearinghouse) must remain matters for speculation, the value of some experimentation in this direction appears clear.

It is interesting, in this connection, that importers tend to think initially in terms of areas rather than individual suppliers as new sources. Singapore, for example, was mentioned as an area several importers (AB and BY) were investigating. While this may hamper the efforts of exporters of other countries to open up American trade contacts, it does suggest a way in which an international clearinghouse could capitalize on the willingness of importers to investigate new areas, by furnishing them with proposals from such areas.

SUMMARY

In looking over the various aspects of the exporter-importer relationship discussed in this study, it has become apparent that many of the marketing problems described could be solved by actions within the exporters' power. It appears, for example, that the technicalities of international trade do not furnish a formidable barrier to the expansion of manufactured imports from the developing countries, although suppliers in some cases need to take certain remedial actions to make their operations more effective in this respect.

Communication problems, on the other hand, do exist, not only in human affairs generally and in business specifically, especially small business, but most importantly in international trade and in new types of trade such as that covered by this study. Face-to-face communication is limited; written communication, because of the expense, tends to be abbreviated; and the exchange of instructions is clouded by the host of linguistic and cultural factors that come between men of different nationalities and cultures.

Cultural differences may be simply matters of manners and custom, or they may represent deep differences in business philosophy. Attitudes toward profits (long range versus short range), toward productive enterprise, and toward competition can all separate the entrepreneur in the developing country from his American importer. And government policies toward private enterprise may play a role in the attitudes of the former.

Importers report that they are cognizant of these problems and yet hope some of the basic ones will be gradually alleviated.

The penetration into the developing country of entrepreneurial thinking on the American pattern supports this hope. Some importers are also interested in bringing their trading partners to the United States, so that the requirements of the importers can be understood right "on the ground" in the American market.

Another specific proposal, generally endorsed by importers contacted on this matter, was for the establishment of some type of international clearinghouse for the presentation of new products. The envisaged clearinghouse would be operated by some type of nonprofit organization, such as the International Trade Center, and its efforts would be addressed to opening up new contacts for suppliers in developing countries. The service is seen as supplementing what must necessarily be the limited efforts of importers themselves to visit the developing countries and establish new sources.

NOTES

1. Joe S. Bain, Barriers to New Competition (Cambridge, Mass.: Harvard University Press, 1956), presents a discussion of "the conditions of entry" to an industry (pp. 1-41) and comments on know-how as an entry factor (p. 148).

2. See, for example, Philip MacDonald, Practical Exporting and Importing (2d ed.; New York: Ronald Press, 1959), Chs. 8, 11, and 12.

3. D. Stikker, The Role of Private Enterprise in Investment and Promotion of Exports in Developing Countries, Document TD/35/ Rev. 1 (New York: United Nations, 1968), p. 80.

4. The intricacies of exporting from some of the developing countries are discussed by Talaat Abdel-Malek, "Import Substitution vs. Export Orientation," Columbia Journal of World Business, September-October, 1969, p. 33: "Bureaucratic machinery and red tape represent another relevant area of government responsibility where progress has been lacking in developing countries. The multiplicity of laws and regulations pertaining to exports, the variety of control agencies, the overlap in their jurisdiction, the occasional inconsistencies and conflicting interpretations of rules, and the lengthy process of documentation are some of the most powerful invisible barriers to export growth."

5. "Because messages can now be sent from continent to

continent and from country to country with ease, many persons assume that communication from man to man can also be accomplished with ease . . . this assumption should not be made too hastily. Man has broken the sound barrier and has crossed many hurdles, but he has not yet learned to overcome the greatest barrier of all—his limited ability to exchange ideas with his fellow man. He tends to be short-sighted, resistant to unfamiliar concepts, skeptical, and on occasion irrational. These reactions are intensified by distances, language and cultural differences, economic variables, and many other factors."
John Enell, Vice President for Research, American Management Association, "Foreword" to Dimitris Chorafas, The Communication Barrier in International Management, Research Study 100 (New York: American Management Association 1969), p. 5.

6. Quoted from United States Reports, 1918, by Wesley Wiksell, Do They Understand You? (New York: Macmillan, 1960), p. 63.

7. Communication in Organizations: Some New Research Findings (Ann Arbor, Mich.: Foundation for Research in Human Behavior, 1959), pp. 5-11.

8. L. J. Crampon, Communicating Information to Small Businessmen (Boulder: University of Colorado Bureau of Business Research, 1964), p. ix.

9. Roy Blough, International Business: Environment and Adaptation (New York: McGraw-Hill Co., 1966), p. 42, puts it this way: "Communication between persons of different cultures is particularly difficult because the unseen, even unconscious assumptions, meanings and images that underlie understanding are so different in different cultures. The special problems of communication in international business are not limited to the difficulties arising from illiteracy and inadequacies of education, . . . There are also the barriers of verbal language and the 'silent language' of manners and customs." Communications problems also beset U.S. exporters. The U.S. Department of Commerce, for example, regularly exhorts American exporters to "quote prices c.i.f." so that overseas purchasers can understand their landed costs.

10. Henry P. deVries, "The Language Barrier," Columbia Journal of World Business, July-August, 1969, p. 79.

11. The very "universality" of English suggests substantial variations in patterns of its use and understanding: Alexander

Ostrower, Language, Law and Diplomacy (Philadelphia: University of Pennsylvania Press, 1965), p. 389, quotes estimates that 500 million people have English either as a mother tongue or as a second language.

12. Glenn A. Bassett, The New Face of Communication (New York: American Management Association, 1968), p. 85.

13. Blough, International Business, p. 7, discusses how time periods in profit expectations affect business decision-making.

14. The paradox of the pro-investment statements of developing countries and their antiprofit actions is capsulized in "Proud Borrower and Shy Investor," from The Economist, reprinted in T. Morgan, G. Betz, and N. K. Choudhry, eds., Readings in Economic Development (Belmont, Calif.: Wadsworth Publishing Co., 1963), pp. 400-403.

15. Eli Ginzberg, "Asian Development: The Achievement of the Possible," Columbia Journal of World Business, July-August, 1969, pp. 86-89, points out that some of the developing countries have a surplus of college graduates available for demanding jobs.

16. Wayne Broehl, Jr., "A Less Developed Entrepreneur," Columbia Journal of World Business, March-April, 1970, pp. 26-34.

17. Wayne Broehl, Jr., The International Basic Economy Corporation (Washington, D.C.: National Planning Association, 1968), pp. 87-96.

18. U.S., Department of Commerce, Bureau of International Commerce, The Market for Food Processing and Packaging Machinery and Equipment in the Philippines, DIB 71 = 08 = 512 (Washington, D.C.: Department of Commerce, Commercial Intelligence Division, October, 1970).

19. World Markets for U.S. Exports: Food Processing, Packaging Equipment, Mexico, IMIS 70 = 207 (Washington, D.C.: U.S. Government Printing Office, May 1970), p. 2.

20. Interview with Dr. H. L. Jacobson, Director of the International Trade Center, Geneva, May 14, 1968.

9

FINDINGS

AND

CONCLUSIONS

FINDINGS

Because of the importance of trade expansion to the economic development of the developing countries and because of the importance of manufactured exports to that expansion, this study has undertaken to analyze certain factors involved in increasing U.S. manufactured imports from such countries. Marketing factors have been the focus of this study. The appropriateness of this focus is supported by the fact that the technology of marketing is highly developed in the United States. Additionally, certain alternative solutions to the problem of export expansion, such as the achievement of larger or deeper capital investments in the developing countries, or the elimination of major official international trade barriers, are subject to strong economic or substantial political constraints. Data for the study were drawn from a variety of sources, but particularly from the experience of the sector of the American business community most directly concerned: American importers.

The study first undertook an examination of the trends in U.S. imports from a selected group of developing countries. It was found that aggregate imports from these countries increased 49 percent between 1964 and 1970, with almost three fourths of the countries participating in this increase. During the same period, however, U.S. total imports increased 115 percent. But the proportion of manufactured products, represented by SITC groups 5 through 8, in these imports has been increasing. In 1964, they were only 17 percent; by 1970, they had reached 28 percent. There is also evidence that imports of processed foods from the developing countries have been increasing.

This apparently beneficial trend has been somewhat counter-balanced by the extreme concentration of manufactured imports from the developing countries in certain categories. Textiles and clothing are of particular significance in this respect; other products forming major portions of the manufactured imports are processed metals and minerals, a limited range of wood products, and footwear. Some of these products share with primary products the problems of demand inelasticity; others, such as footwear and textiles, have grown so rapidly as to threaten protectionist reactions in the United States, as well as in other developed country markets.

Next, the study undertook an analysis of the nature of demand patterns for manufactured imports from the developing countries. A distinction was drawn between price and nonprice factors in this demand, and the importance of product differentiation in making possible nonprice demand influences was emphasized. The current high level of U.S. tariffs was considered as a demand influence, and it was concluded that the possible reductions in landed costs from tariff reduction or elimination are rather limited. The actions that sellers might take in the event of tariff reductions (or increases) were considered, and the feasibility of nonprice competition was emphasized in this regard.

The importance of the trading relationship rather than the individual transaction in imports of manufactured products from the developing countries was examined, and a theoretical presentation was offered to depict this relationship.

The likelihood that the concentration of manufactured imports from the developing countries in certain product categories is due at least in major part to the lack of diversified marketing know-how was considered. It presently appears that correction of this lack can have very beneficial effects on expanding manufactured imports from the developing countries.

The importance of design in its total sense—i.e., in the conception of the product, rather than in the treatment of its external aspects—was next explored. Statistical and qualitative evidence was offered as to the unusual degree to which American consumers have purchase options beyond what may be considered necessities. Marketers were found constantly to be able to cater to such options, some of which they themselves help to create. Nonetheless, this opportunity is fraught with some peril: what the marketer proposes, the market can dispose of. The mortality of product design was found to be particularly swift in the case of such products as fashion goods, and

the need accordingly becomes paramount for the importer and exporter to work closely together in such areas.

A classification of designs into distinctive-purpose, distinctive-
image, and accepted-image categories was proposed. The first two
categories can bring great rewards to innovators, but most imports
of manufactured goods from the developing countries doubtlessly fall
into the last category. A willingness on the part of the supplier in
the developing country to make the necessary design modifications in
his product was found to be of prime importance to U.S. importers.
The importance of subcontract-type industrial imports was discussed.

A marketing opportunity was found to stem from the disillusionment of the American consumer with the quality of the products he is
currently purchasing. In the past, Americans have rated imported
products at both the top and the bottom of the quality scale, but the
Japanese post-World War II experience has demonstrated that a
country can change the quality image of its products in the American
market.

The issue of quality control was examined, and it was found that
quality, rather than depending on complex equipment or sophisticated
techniques, sometimes may be more a matter of certain management
skills, particularly the concern for quality itself. Quality marks or
certifications were found to have importance in some instances, but
it was suggested that a quality mark, used by exporters, should, if it
is to have a marketing impact, be adequately supported by actual
testing and control. Specification standards used in the United States
may have anything from a slight to a major impact on the marketing
of manufactured imports, and importer guidance in this field is
essential.

It was suggested that consumerism—a new concern by Americans
about the quality of their environment and the goods they purchase—
can be turned to the advantage of suppliers of manufactured goods
from the developing countries by studying the resultant changes in
market demand, and catering to them.

Next, the study turned to the problem of packing and packaging.
Both these tasks present problems in countries where previous experience may be largely limited to conventional ways of preparing
primary products for international shipment. Packing difficulties
were found to include shortages of materials as well as know-how,
but importers expressed the desire that, above all, their suppliers
show adequate concern for packing their shipments to assure safe

arrival. Packaging problems were found to extend beyond those of material and technical know-how: the distinctive selling role of the package in America's predominantly self-service form of retailing imposes a unique requirement on overseas suppliers. Repackaging of products imported in bulk was found to be frequently too costly to be practical. Unpackaged products are likely to be confined to limited channels of distribution. Suppliers of manufactured products in developing countries are more likely to be able to "sell the product" rather than the brand in their packaging. Private-brand merchandise was found to typify this approach in the American market.

Currently, American packagers are striving for the somewhat contrary goals of low-cost techniques and high-convenience packaging. Some of the techniques in use are highly mechanized, but imported products may be able to compete if they have at least basic package features. Particularly pressing is the need of the supplier in the developing country to be fully acquainted with laws and regulations applying to packaging and labeling, which range from requirements for printing the name of the maker or the distributor on the package to "voluntary" programs curbing package proliferation.

Issues involved in the distribution of manufactured imports from the developing countries were examined. Importers were found to fall into three general groupings: specialist importers, import operations of mass-merchandising organizations, and importers bringing in products for their own industrial use. Among the problems in selecting importers is the vastness of the American market, which requires even some of the country's largest companies to segment their marketing efforts. Certain suggestions were made as to how the market for an imported manufactured product from the developing countries could be usefully segmented. Decisions, however, would have to be a matter of candid exchange of views between exporter and importer.

Certain apparently undesirable marketing practices by suppliers in developing countries were specified. One of these was the failure by a supplier to grant his importer some degree of exclusivity within the importer's market. A second was the sale of the same product to different levels of distribution within the United States without respect to price differences traditionally associated with each level of distribution.

The particular requirements of sales promotion were next dealt with. Notwithstanding the crucial importance of such promotion to success in the American market, the consensus of importers was that it should be left in their hands. The knowledge and the skills are theirs. The basic tool required for their efforts is a landed cost sufficiently low to leave room for their promotional expenditures.

Finally, the study delved into the question of why many of the foregoing factors, though presumably largely under the control of the exporter in the developing country, are not handled in the way that they should be for maximum effectiveness in expanding trade. An incidental inquiry along this route was whether this failure to perform with maximum effectiveness was linked to an inability on the part of suppliers in the developing countries to cope with certain of the technicalities of international trade, such as documentation and shipping arrangements. American importers were found to think not.

Instead, it appears that communication failures—characteristic of all business affairs, but particularly difficult in this novel type of international trade—bear a substantial portion of the blame. These problems range from the obvious ones of language to the complex matter of business philosophy and are in some cases complicated by the attitudes of government in the developing countries.

Importers nonetheless are optimistic. They do what they can to alleviate communication gaps, traveling frequently to visit their sources, for example. It was suggested that an even better solution would be for source representatives to visit the American market and view its operation for themselves. Also suggested, and favorably commented on by a number of American importers, was a proposal for some sort of nonprofit international clearinghouse, to serve as a channel for the development of new sources of supply for importers. The GATT/UNCTAD International Trade Center in Geneva might be a suitable sponsor. While the idea would be applicable to markets in all of the industrialized countries, it might be of special value to certain suppliers in the developing countries who hesitate to enter the great American market.

To illustrate some of the possible practical applications of certain of the preceding findings, Figure 2 has been prepared. The figure, addressed to the supplier or potential supplier of manufactured imports from a developing country, raises questions that may enable such a firm to avoid possible pitfalls in its American marketing efforts.

FIGURE 2

Checklist for Screening American Market Opportunities for
Manufactured Exports from the Developing Countries

DESIGN

Can you furnish a product for "the man who has everything," i.e., a new type of purchase option?

Or can you supply fresh inspiration, based on your country's designs, for something already in popular use in the United States?

Can you adapt your product to what the American importer says his market requires?

Or can you handle an exact-specification "subcontract" for an industrial importer?

QUALITY

Can you offer a product of a high enough quality to attract buyers who find home-market quality disappointing?

Are you managing your plant to get quality products through the efforts of your staff, rather than simply depending on your equipment?

Can you obtain the use of a mark or symbol that denotes quality?

Have you consulted with your American importer to avoid problems with consumerism laws and regulations in the U.S.?.

PACKAGING

Are you sure that your packing will deliver the product safely to the importer?

Can you package it for retail sale?

Have you a package design that will sell?

Does your labeling meet U.S. requirements?

DISTRIBUTION

Do you understand the requirements of the type of importer you are selling to, e.g., specialist, mass-merchandiser, or industrial buyer?

Have you worked out with your importer or importers how the American market for your product will be covered?

Do you avoid competing with your importer or importers by letting them make the sales in their territories?

CONCLUSIONS

The picture that emerges from an examination of the importation
of manufactured products from the developing countries is not that
of a broad, homogeneous market ebbing and flowing with the tides of
competition. Instead, one sees a series of highly individualized types
of products, channels, transactions, and participants, whose relationships are governed by the substantial intricacies of individualized
marketing relationships. These relationships are susceptible to
improvement in a variety of ways, all of which offer promise of expanding the trade involved.

One way of looking at this matter is to view it in terms of
what Americans today call the "marketing concept."[1] In general, the
marketing concept is defined by American marketing experts as a
concentration on the customer: research and analysis of his habits,
his needs, his wants, and then development of the most effective ways
of catering to these buying factors. Within the United States, the
focus of the marketing concept is on the final buyer.

But the distance, both spatial and institutional, that separates
the supplier in the developing country and most final buyers in the
United States makes this use of the marketing concept difficult.
Instead, the supplier may well concentrate on the American importer,
viewing him qua final buyer. It is largely the voice of the American
importer that has been heard on these pages. He speaks, of course,
for the final buyer for whom his sales are destined; because his
existence depends on effectively serving that final buyer, his counsels
can be used most advantageously by the supplier in the developing
country.

Specific steps to be taken by the supplier to serve his importer-
customer better emerge fairly clearly from the foregoing study.
First, the importer wants a greater variety of things. He has been
served well in such products as textiles and shoes, but he will buy a
host of additional products if they are offered to him, ranging from
industrial fabrications to home furnishings. Second, he is hungrily
seeking new designs—and sometimes this means literally new kinds
of products—to offer to the restless, always-available optional tastes
of the American public. Third, he needs help in building permanent
customers by offering them a product whose quality per dollar compares effectively with what the increasingly critical American final
buyer can get elsewhere. Fourth, he wants not only packing that
delivers the product safe to his door but, if at all possible, packaging

that moves it off the shelves and into the hands of final buyers without personal selling. Finally, he wants to be treated fairly with respect to the distributive practices of his supplier. This means giving him a definite territory in which to sell and, if selling is to be undertaken at other levels of distribution, adjusting prices accordingly, so that some small-volume buyer, for example, is not paying as little per unit as does the large-volume importer.

To do all of these things, and do them well, requires a conscious concentration on the flow of communication between the supplier in the developing country and the American importer. The supplier needs to strive for an understanding of the special requirements of his importer-customer with respect to such matters as delivery. If he can visit the United States to observe these matters firsthand, he is perhaps undertaking one of the best types of market research available.

Assuming, then, that certain conditions that will promote expansion of manufactured imports from the developing countries have been isolated and described, what is the likelihood that these conditions will be fulfilled within the near future? They are certainly promising to some extent. The demonstrated success of textile and shoe exporters in the developing countries, for example, should encourage efforts to develop markets for additional manufactured exports. Then, too, certain organizations, such as Japanese trading companies, well schooled in export to the United States, now include in their operations export from some of the developing countries to the United States. They, too, can demonstrate how the job can be done effectively. Finally, if, as has been predicted, the multinational companies will increasingly base production operations in the developing countries, they will also export successfully to the United States, since they already are effective marketers there.

Beyond this, what can one hope for? Since, as has been mentioned in Chapter 1, the governments of developing countries have made it their national purpose to promote exports of manufactured products, can they be of help in educating their exporters to the requirements of the American market? The answer undoubtedly is that they can be of great help in many instances. In cases in which such governments have joined with the United States in export marketing projects in connection with U.S. foreign-assistance efforts, significant results appear to have been achieved.[2] Ill-considered export promotion efforts, on the other hand, may have a negative rather than a positive effect, as has been mentioned in connection with certain export incentive schemes in which the procedures and

standards have become so complex as to act as a barrier rather
than an inducement to a new type of export.

Government influence on the economies of the developing countries is generally so all-pervasive that a simple awareness on the
part of government leaders of the marketing requirements for exports
can have a salutary effect. The case in Chapter 5, for example, in
which government permission was needed to arrange for the importation of satisfactory thread, illustrates how the little things may
become the big things in the marketing of manufactured exports.

Simply a willingness on the part of the government to explore
the opportunities for improved marketing knowledge for its exporters
may be of great importance. Resources for assistance may be right
at hand. Although the traditional type of U.S. foreign assistance is
currently largely being phased out, new proposals for U.S. participa-
tion in efforts related to economic development have already been
made.[3] Here, there may be a new emphasis on multilateral types
of aid, such as those through the United Nations and its affiliated
agencies.

The International Trade Center offers an excellent example of
a multilateral type of marketing assistance that has probably been
inadequately exploited in making the American market more understandable and approachable to suppliers of manufactured products
in developing countries. A clearinghouse, of the type proposed by
an American importer (see Chapter 8) would doubtlessly be an excellent extension of the Center's activities. The uniqueness of the
plan might have the special value of focusing world attention on marketing aspects as a way of promoting manufactured exports.

At this point, it is appropriate to turn back to the comment
made at the end of Chapter 3 to the effect that the increase in certain
types of manufactured imports from the developing countries might
provoke political reactions in the United States in the form of restrictive legislation. Although, as this is written, quota issues are
clouded by the presence of the 10 percent import surcharge, proposals
for new quotas on such products as noncotton textiles, shoes, and
perhaps other products are likely eventually to make their reappear-
ance.

It is suggested that the thrust of the findings and recommendations of this study should ameliorate rather than exacerbate this
situation. The reason that a knife cuts is that, when even moderate
force is applied to the very limited area represented by a sharp edge,

a tremendous pressure is exerted at the point of contact; so it is with manufactured imports that have an impact on a very limited area of American industry. If, on the other hand, the lack of diversified marketing understanding referred to in Chapter 3 can be remedied, then the imports from developing countries can be spread over wide areas of the economy, with consequent greatly limited impact on any one of them. The resulting inducements to developing-country exporters to open new fields can considerably reduce the quota pressure in the fields now subject to heavy exploitation.

What the entire question boils down to is whether the typical producer or would-be producer of a manufactured product in the developing country can achieve the necessary marketing-concept understanding of his American customer, the U.S. importer. Everything that can help in this direction—further efforts on the part of the importer himself, sympathetic aid from the developing-country government (perhaps helped through bilateral or multilateral technical assistance), and perhaps the opportunity of the exporter himself to visit the American market so that he can personally see the nature of that market—all of these things, by contributing in their way to better marketing, should contribute to expanded imports by the United States of manufactured products from the developing countries. This in its own way offers one more hope for progress, growth, and tranquility in this still very troubled world.

NOTES

1. Theodore Beckman and William Davidson, Marketing (8th ed.; New York: Ronald Press, 1967), p. 41, characterize the emergence of the marketing concept in the following terms: "In general, this transition has been from emphasis on selling what a company has to the producing of goods and services that are wanted by customers." Philip Kotler, Marketing Management (Englewood Cliffs, N.J.: Prentice-Hall, 1967), p. 3, attributes the marketing concept to the fact that in the United States "the . . . present stage of the economy is marked not by a scarcity of goods, but by a scarcity of markets."

2. See, for example, Amicus Most, Expanding Imports: A Case Study of the Korean Experience (Washington, D.C.: U.S. Agency for International Development, 1969).

3. In March, 1970, a Presidential Task Force headed by R. A. Peterson called for a reorientation of U.S. foreign assistance, including greater emphasis on both loans and multilateral aid. New York

<u>Times</u>, March 1, 1970, p. 1, col. 3. See also <u>U.S. Foreign Assistance</u>
<u>in the 1970's: A New Approach</u>, Report to the President from the
Task Force on International Development (Washington, D.C.: U.S.
Government Printing Office, March 4, 1970).

APPENDIXES

TYPES OF PRODUCTS HANDLED BY, AND REGIONAL LOCATION OF, FIRMS CONTACTED IN THIS STUDY

Identification*	Location	Types of Products
AA	New York	n.a.
AB	California	Sporting goods, novelties
AC	California	Consumer products
AD	New York	Glass and crystal
AE	New York	Food products
AF	Massachusetts	Footwear
AG	New Jersey	Art materials
AH	Pennsylvania	Gift and housewares
AJ	New York	Mass merchandiser
AK	Illinois	Decorative products
AL	New York	Cutlery
AM	New York	Textile products
AN	New York	Hair products
AP	New York	Flatware
AQ	California	Specialty products
AR	New York	Cosmetic products
AS	New York	Metal products
AT	New York	n.a.
AU	New York	Textile products
AV	New York	Textile products
AW	New York	Alcoholic beverages
AX	Ohio	n.a.
AY	New York	Footwear

Identification	Location	Types of Products
AZ	New York	Housewares
BA	New York	Apparel products
BB	New York	Food products
BC	New York	Bicycle products
BD	New York	Musical instruments
BE	Rhode Island	Jewelry
BF	New York	Consumer and industrial products
BG	New York	Crystal
BH	New York	Mass merchandiser
BJ	Illinois	Apparel products
BK	Massachusetts	Giftware
BL	New York	Toys
BM	New York	Housewares
BN	New York	Floor coverings
BP	New York	Mass merchandiser
BQ	Illinois	Food products
BR	New York	Mass merchandiser
BS	New York	Apparel products
BT	New York	Store fixtures
BU	New York	Mass merchandiser
BV	New York	Consumer and industrial products
BW	New York	Floor coverings
BX	Connecticut	n.a.
BY	New York	Decorative products
BZ	New York	Toys and decorative products
CA	New York	Industrial products
CB	New York	Glassware
CC	New York	Toys
CD	New York	Glass products
CE	New York	Apparel products
CF	New York	Headware
CG	New York	Toys
CH	New York	Housewares
CJ	New York	Giftware
CK	New York	Furniture
CL	New York	Hair products
CN	California	Food products
CP	California	Costume apparel
CQ	California	Floor coverings
CR	California	Consumer and industrial products

Identification	Location	Types of Products
CS	New York	Mass merchandiser
CT	California	Food products
CU	New York	Apparel products
PA**	Philippines	Wood products
PB**	Philippines	Handicrafts

---

*Identification numbers are used in text and footnotes. Except as noted, all firms contacted were importers.

**Exporter.

APPENDIX FIGURE 1

Theoretical Effect of Cost Reduction Stemming from Preferential Tariff Reduction on Supply-Demand-Price Relationships Under Perfect Competition

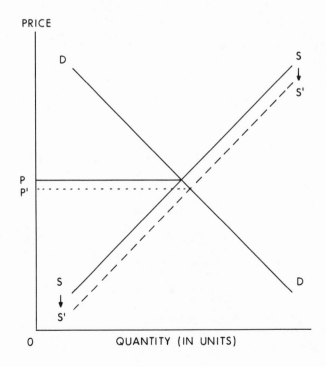

Appendix Figure 1 depicts the intersection of demand and supply, with D-D representing demand and S-S representing the supply (at landed duty-paid costs) before the tariff reduction. S'-S' represents a new supply schedule after tariff reduction, with the arrows depicting the amount of the tariff removed. If the developing-country suppliers do not change their prices, they would supply the same amount of product at prices lower than the former landed costs by the amount of this tariff reduction.

The developing-country suppliers, however, are presumably not the only suppliers; part of the market is probably served from other countries and by domestic suppliers. Because the costs of these suppliers have not been reduced, the average cost of all suppliers is decreased by less than the amount of the tariff reduction, and the new market price is therefore somewhere between P and P'.

Two effects can be readily deduced. First, demand, for which the schedule has not been changed, is increased by the lower price. Second, since the price reduction will be lower than the tariff reduction, the new landed duty-paid price will offer a higher net price to exporters in the developing countries. This should induce additional supplies from exporters in such countries, including suppliers in countries from which the United States has not previously received such imports.

BIBLIOGRAPHY

Abbott, Lawrence. Quality and Competition. New York: Columbia
    University Press, 1955.

Baily, Nathan, ed. Marketing Profitably Under the Robinson-Patman
    Act. Washington, D.C.: Public Affairs Press, 1963.

Bain, Joe S. Barriers to New Competition. Cambridge, Mass.: Harvard
    University Press, 1956.

Bassett, Glenn A. The New Face of Communication. New York:
    American Management Association, 1968.

Beckman, Theodore; and Davidson, William. Marketing. 8th ed.
    New York: Ronald Press, 1967.

Bliss, Perry, ed. Marketing and the Behavioral Sciences. Boston:
    Allyn and Bacon, Inc., 1963.

Blough, Roy. International Business: Environment and Adaptation.
    New York: McGraw-Hill Co., 1966.

Borden, N., Jr. Acceptance of New Food Products by Supermarkets.
    Boston: Harvard University Press, 1968.

Brand, E. A. Modern Supermarket Operation. New York: Fairchild
    Publications, 1963.

Britt, Steuart The Spenders. New York: McGraw-Hill, 1960.

Broehl, Wayne, Jr. The International Basic Economy Corporation.
    Washington, D.C.: National Planning Association, 1968.

Bryce, Murray. Policies and Methods for Industrial Development.
    New York: McGraw-Hill, 1965.

Carson, Rachel. Silent Spring. Boston: Houghton Mifflin, 1962.

The Case for Good Design. New York: American Management
    Association, 1963.

Chamberlin, Edward. Theory of Monopolistic Competition. 2d ed.
    Cambridge, Mass.: Harvard University Press, 1936.

Chorafas, Dimitris. The Communication Barrier in International
    Management. Research Study 100. New York: American Man-
    agement Association, 1969.

Commission for the International Bank for Reconstruction and Development. Partners in Development New York: Praeger, 1969.

Communication in Organizations: Some New Research Findings. Ann Arbor, Mich.: Foundation for Research in Human Behavior, 1959.

Crampon, L. J. Communicating Information to Small Businessmen. Boulder: University of Colorado Bureau of Business Research, 1964.

DeVries, B. A. The Export Experience of Developing Countries. International Bank for Reconstruction and Development Occasional Paper No. 3. Baltimore, Md.: Johns Hopkins Press, 1967.

Diamond, William. Distribution Channels for Industrial Goods. Monograph 114. Columbus: Ohio State University, Bureau of Business Research, 1963.

Directory of Ohio Manufacturers, 1961. Columbus: State of Ohio Department of Industrial Relations, 1961.

Directory of Texas Manufacturers, 1962. Austin: University of Texas Bureau of Business Research, 1962.

Distribution des Biens de Consommation en Amérique du Nord. Paris: Comité Franc-Dollar, October, 1967.

Dreyfuss, Henry. Designing for People. New York: Simon and Schuster, 1955.

Dun and Bradstreet. Middle Market Directory, 1971. New York, 1970.

_____. Million Dollar Directory, 1970. New York, 1970.

du Pont de Nemours, E. I., & Company. Consumer Buying Habits Studies. Wilmington, Del., 1965.

Engel, James; Kollat, David; and Blackwell, Roger Consumer Behavior. New York: Holt, Rinehart and Winston, 1968.

Field, G. A.; Douglas, J.; and Tarpey, L. X. Marketing Management: A Behavioral Systems Approach. Columbus, Ohio: Merrill Books, Inc., 1966.

Galbraith, J. K. Economic Development in Perspective. Cambridge, Mass.: Harvard University Press, 1962.

Galenson, Walter, ed. Labor and Economic Development. New York: Wiley, 1959.

_____. Labor in Developing Economies. Berkeley: University of California Press, 1962.

General Agreement on Tariffs and Trade. International Trade 1967-69. Geneva: Secretariat of the Contacting Parties, 1968, 1969, 1970.

Goldenthal, Irving. How to Plan Stocks, Sales and Open-to-buy. Philadelphia: Chilton Co., 1953.

Guss, L. M. Packaging Is Marketing. New York: American Management Association, 1967.

Hamilton, David. The Consumer in Our Economy. Boston: Houghton Mifflin, 1962.

Hilton, Peter. Keeping Old Products New. Englewood Cliffs, N.J.: Prentice-Hall, 1967.

Holloway, R. J. and Hancock, R. S. Marketing in a Changing Environment. New York: John Wiley & Sons, 1968.

Hunsberger, Warren. Japan and the United States in World Trade. New York: Harper & Row, 1964.

International Trade Center. The Role of the Freight Forwarder in Developing Countries. Geneva: UNCATD/GATT, 1969.

Jarnow, Jeannette, and Judelle, Beatrice. Inside the Fashion Business. New York: John Wiley and Sons, 1965.

Katona, George, et al. The Mass Consumption Society. New York: McGraw-Hill, 1964.

Kerr, Clark, et al. Industrialization and Industrial Man. Cambridge, Mass.: Harvard University Press, 1960.

Kotler, Philip. Marketing Management. Englewood Cliffs, N.J.: Prentice-Hall, 1967.

Lary, H. B. Imports of Manufactures from Less Developed Countries. New York: National Bureau of Economic Research, 1968.

Levin, Jonathan The Export Economies. Cambridge, Mass.: Harvard University Press, 1960.

Lewis, H. T.; Willton, J. W.; and Stelle, J. D. The Role of Air Freight in Physical Distribution. Boston: Graduate School of Business Administration, Harvard University, 1956.

McCarthy, E. J. Basic Marketing: A Managerial Approach. 3d ed. Homewood, Ill.: R. D. Irwin, Inc., 1968.

MacDonald, Morgan, Jr. Appraising the Market for New Industrial Products. Business Policy Study No. 123. New York: National Industrial Conference Board, 1967.

MacDonald, Philip. Practical Exporting and Importing. 2d ed. New York: Ronald Press, 1959.

Magnuson, W. G., and Carper, Jean. The Dark Side of the Marketplace. Englewood Cliffs, N.J.: Prentice-Hall, 1968.

Maizels, Alfred. Industrial Growth and World Trade. London: Cambridge University Press, 1963.

Mandelbaum, K. The Industrialization of Backward Areas. Oxford: Basil Blackwell, 1947.

Marketing Research Report on Packaging. New York: American Management Association, 1957.

Melnitsky, Benjamin. Profiting from Industrial Standardization. New York: Conover-Mast Publications, 1953.

Missouri Directory of Manufacturers. 1966 ed. Jefferson City: Missouri Division of Commercial and Industrial Development, 1968.

Modern Packaging Encyclopedia. New York: McGraw-Hill, July, 1969.

T. Morgan, G. Betz, and N. K. Choudhry, eds. Readings in Economic Development. Belmont, Calif.: Wadsworth Publishing Co., 1963.

Most, Amicus. Expanding Imports: A Case Study of the Korean Experience. Washington, D.C.: U.S. Agency for International Development, 1969.

Mountjoy, Alan. Industrialization and Under-Developed Countries.
    London: Hutchinson University Library, 1963.

Moyer, Reed. Marketing in Economic Development. East Lansing:
    Institute for International Business Management Studies, Michigan
    State University, Occasional Paper No. 1, 1965.

Nader, Ralph. Unsafe at Any Speed. New York: Grossman, 1965.

National Industrial Conference Board. Expenditure Patterns of the
    American Family. New York, 1965.

_____. Organization for New Product Development. New York,
    1966.

1968 California Manufacturers Directory. Los Angeles: Times
    Mirror Press, 1968.

1967 Annual New Jersey State Industrial Directory. New York, 1962.

Olson, C. J. and Ellis, R. C. Export or Die. Chicago: Dartnell, 1966.

Organization for Economic Cooperation and Development. Trade by
    Commodities—Market Summaries. Series C, Vol. I: General,
    January-December 1969. Paris, 1970.

Ostrower, Alexander. Language, Law and Diplomacy. Philadelphia:
    University of Pennsylvania Press, 1965.

Oxenfeldt, Alfred. Executive Action in Marketing. Belmont, Calif.:
    Wadsworth Publishing Co., 1966.

Package Design and Its Management. New York: American Manage-
    ment Association, 1965.

Packaging Considerations for the Marketing Man. New York: American
    Management Association, 1966.

Phillipps, Charles F., and Duncan, Delbert J. Marketing Principles
    and Methods. 6th ed. Homewood, Ill.: R. D. Irwin, 1968.

Pincus, J. Trade, Aid and Development. New York: McGraw-Hill,
    1967.

Preeg, Ernest. Traders and Diplomats. Washington, D.C.: The
    Brookings Institution, 1970.

Profitability and Penetration Through Packaging. New York: American Management Association, 1965.

Rewoldt, S. H.; Scott, J. D.; and Warshaw, M. R. Introduction to Marketing Management. Homewood, Ill.: R. D. Irwin, 1969.

Robinson, Joan. Economics of Imperfect Competition. London: Macmillan, 1934.

Rostow, W. W. The Stages of Economic Growth. Cambridge, Eng.: The University Press, 1967.

Stigler, George. The Theory of Competitive Price. New York: Macmillan, 1942.

Stikker, D. The Role of Private Enterprise in Investment and Promotion of Exports in Developing Countries. Document TD/35/Rev. 1. New York: United Nations, 1968.

Struglia, E. J. Standards and Specifications: Information Sources. Management Information Guide 6. Detroit: Gale Research Co., 1965.

Taylor, W. J., and Shaw, R. T., Jr. Marketing: An Integrated Analytical Approach. 2d ed. Cincinnati, Ohio: South-Western Publishing Co., 1969.

United Nations Conference on Trade and Development. Trade in Manufactures, VI. New York, 1964.

United Nations. Yearbook of International Statistics, 1967. New York, 1969.

U.S. Bureau of the Census. City and County Data Book 1967. Washington, D.C.: U.S. Government Printing Office, 1967.

_____. Current Population Reports. "Poverty in the United States: 1959 and 1968," Series P-60, No. 68. Washington, D.C.: U.S. Government Printing Office, 1969.

_____. 1967 Census of Manufactures: Grain Mill Products. MC67(20)-20D. Washington, D.C.: U.S. Government Printing Office, 1970.

_____. Publication Program, 1967 Census of Manufactures and Mineral Industries. Washington, D.C., January, 1970.

_____. U.S. Census of Population: 1960. Detailed Characteristics, California PC(1)-6D. Washington, D.C.: U.S. Government Printing Office, 1962.

_____. U.S. Census of Population: 1960. Detailed Characteristics, U.S. Summary PC(1)-ID. Washington, D.C.: U.S. Government Printing Office, 1963.

_____. U.S. Census of Population, 1960. Subject Reports: Persons of Spanish Surname PC(2)-B. Washington, D.C.: U.S. Government Printing Office, 1963.

_____. U.S. General Imports. Report FT 155. 1968 and 1970 Annual. Washington, D.C.: U.S. Government Printing Office, 1969, 1971.

_____. U.S. Imports of Merchandise for Consumption. Report FT 125, December, 1964. Washington, D.C.: U.S. Government Printing Office, 1965.

U.S. Bureau of Customs. Exporting to the United States. Washington, D.C.: U.S. Government Printing Office, 1963.

U.S. Congress. Senate. Committee on Finance. Steel Imports, S. Rept., 90th Cong., 1st sess. Washington, D.C.: U.S. Government Printing Office, 1967.

U.S. Defense Supply Agency. Preservation, Packaging, and Packing of Military Supplies and Equipment. DSAM 4145.2, Vol. II. Washington, D.C., October, 1967.

U.S. Department of Agriculture. Official U.S. Standards for Grades of Carcass Beef. Washington, D.C.: Department of Agriculture Consumer and Marketing Service S.R.A. 99, June, 1965. [Reprint of 1926 issue.]

U.S. Department of Commerce. Report to the Congress by the Secretary of Commerce on Activities Under the Fair Packaging and Labeling Act During Fiscal Year 1968. Washington, D.C.: Department of Commerce, 1968 (?).

U.S. Department of Commerce. Bureau of International Commerce. Basic Data on the Economy of Australia. OBR 63-38. Washington: U.S. Government Printing Office, 1963.

_____. Basic Data on the Economy of Canada. OBR 67-98. Washington, D.C.: U.S. Government Printing Office, December, 1967.

_____. Basic Data on the Economy of Denmark. OBR 68-84.
Washington: U.S. Government Printing Office, 1968.

_____. The Market for Food Processing and Packaging Machinery
and Equipment in the Philippines. DIB 71-08-512. Washington,
D.C.: Department of Commerce Commercial Intelligence
Division, October, 1970.

_____. World Markets for U.S. Exports: Food Processing, Packag-
ing Equipment, Mexico. IMIS 70-207. Washington, D.C.: U.S.
Government Printing Office, May, 1970.

U.S. Department of Commerce. Business and Defense Services Administration. U.S. Industrial Outlook, 1969. Washington, D.C.:
U.S. Government Printing Office, 1968.

U.S. Department of Commerce. National Bureau of Standards.
Directory of U.S. Standardization Activities. Washington, D.C.:
U.S. Government Printing Office, 1967.

U.S. Department of Commerce. Office of Business Economics. Input-
Output Structure of the U.S. Economy: 1963. 3 vols. Washington,
U.S. Government Printing Office, 1969.

U.S. Department of Labor. How American Buying Habits Change.
Washington, D.C.: U.S. Government Printing Office, 1959.

U.S. Department of Labor. Bureau of Labor Statistics. Consumer
Cooperatives. Bulletin 1211. Washington, D.C.: U.S. Government
Printing Office, 1957.

U.S. Federal Trade Commission. Guides for Advertising Allowances
and Other Merchandising Payments and Services. Washington,
D.C., 1969.

_____. Proposed Guide Concerning Use of the Word "Free" and
Similar Representations. Washington, D.C., March 20, 1969.

U.S. Federal Trade Commission. Rules, Regulations, Statement of
General Policy or Interpretation and Exemptions Under the
Fair Packaging and Labeling Act. Washington, D.C.: 1969.

_____. Trade Practice Rules for Household Furniture. Washington,
D.C., December 18, 1963.

U.S. Foreign Assistance in the 1970's: A New Approach. Report to
    the President from the Task Force on International Development.
    Washington, D.C.: U.S. Government Printing Office, March 4,
    1970.

U.S. Small Business Administration. Design is Your Business.
    Washington, D.C.: U.S. Government Printing Office, 1953.

U.S. Tariff Commission. Economic Factors Affecting the Use of
    Items 807.00 and 806.30 of the Tariff Schedules of the United
    States. Investigation 332-61. Washington, D.C.: U.S. Tariff
    Commission, September, 1970.

_____. Olives: Report on Investigation 332-51. Washington: U.S.
    Tariff Commission, 1967.

_____. Quantitative Import Restrictions of the United States.
    Washington, D.C.: Tariff Commission Publication 243, 1968.

_____. Summaries of Trade and Tariff Information. 48 vols.
    Washington, D.C., 1966-71.

Wallace, Don. Shaping America's Products. New York: Reinhold,
    1956.

Wasson, C. R., and McConaughy, D. H. Buying Behavior and Marketing
    Decisions. New York: Appleton-Century-Crofts, 1968.

Weintraub, Sidney. Trade Preferences for Less-Developed Countries.
    New York: Praeger, 1966.

Wiksell, Wesley. Do They Understand You? New York: Macmillan,
    1960.

Wingate, J. W. and Schaller, E. O. Techniques of Retail Merchandising.
    Englewood Cliffs, N.J.: Prentice-Hall, 1956.

World Bank Atlas. Washington, D.C.: International Bank for Recon-
    struction and Development, 1969.

World Almanac, 1969. New York: Newspaper Enterprise Association,
    1968.

Yamey, B. S. "Resale Price Maintenance," in the International Ency-
    clopedia of the Social Sciences. New York: Macmillan Company
    and Free Press, 1968.

ALBERT H. SMALL, Special Assistant for Program Coordination to the U.S. Department of Commerce Export Development Activities Program, has served in a series of responsible positions connected with the international trade field over the past two decades in the Department of Commerce, the Department of State, and the Tariff Commission.

In addition, Dr. Small has had extensive experience as a consultant to private industry in the market-research field. He has also lectured in market research and international business at the American University in Washington, D.C. Dr. Small received his A.B. in economics from Brooklyn College and his A.M. and Ph.D. degrees from the American University. Articles by Dr. Small on trade matters have appeared in such publications as the <u>Columbia Journal of World Business</u>, <u>MSU Business Topics</u>, the <u>International Trade Forum</u>, and <u>Law and Policy in International Business</u>; reprints of his writings have appeared in Japan, India, and Latin America.

Dr. Small chaired the government's interagency subcommittee that recommended the enactment of modernized tariff legislation in 1962 and subsequently served on four U.S. delegations to the General Agreement on Tariffs and Trade in Geneva. More recently, official assignments in the export-promotion field have taken him to the Far East.